The only person who can determine my destiny
is one who can give me everything I need.
That person is only myself and no one else"

-Everest Siwira 2017-

The Long Trip To Canada
Copyright © 2017 by Everest Siwira
No part of this publication may be reproduced,
distributed, or transmitted in any form or by any means,
including photocopying, recording, or other electronic
or mechanical methods, without the prior written
permission of the author, except in the case of brief
quotations embodied in critical reviews and certain
other non-commercial uses permitted by copyright law.

tellwell

Tellwell Talent
www.tellwell.ca
ISBN
978-1-77370-536-1 (Hardcover)
978-1-77370-535-4 (Paperback)
978-1-77370-537-8 (eBook)

The Long Trip To Canada

Everest Siwira

TABLE OF CONTENTS

Chapter One
Celebrating Canadian Citizenship 1

Chapter Two
Making the Decision – Year 2000 7

Chapter Three
Preparations 33

Chapter Four
Stranded in Ghana 51

Chapter Five
Welcome to North America 79

Chapter Six
Arrival in Calgary 95

Chapter Seven
Work Permit Application 111

Chapter Eight
Arrival in The United Kingdom 149

Chapter Nine
The Big Blow! Was it Coincidence? 165

Chapter Ten
The Interview that Never Happened 175

Chapter Eleven
Canada! Here We come! 199

Acknowledgements 211

About the Author 212

Chapter One

Celebrating Canadian Citizenship

Three years had gone by since Zvina and his family had first immigrated to Canada. They had landed in Vancouver and stayed with Zvina's friend Muko. Zvina got a job at a gold mining company research centre where Muko also worked. Three months after arriving, they were blessed with a baby son, Bobo. It was a very difficult time for them since they had no relatives close by to help them through this transition, but they pulled through. After eighteen months in Vancouver, they moved to Trail, BC where Zvina got a job at a smelter. At that time, Jill started studying for her pharmacist registration examinations. After passing both federal and provincial examinations, Jill was registered and she started working at a local pharmacy in Trail. During his second year in Trail, Zvina was approached by a headhunter and offered a job in Fort McMurray, Alberta. At first, Zvina had turned down the offer because he was happy at the smelter. However, the headhunter kept trying to persuade Zvina to take the offer by increasing the salary as well as the signing bonus. Finally, Zvina accepted the offer and they moved to Fort McMurray.

On the morning of September 25th, 2007, Zvina and his family flew to Kelowna, BC. They would be driving to Grand Forks to attend their citizenship ceremony on this momentous day.

When they landed in Kelowna, they rented a car and drove to the city for breakfast. While they were having breakfast at an A&W restaurant, an old man approached their table. He started talking to Bobo.

"Hi, little man!" said the old man. "Are you enjoying your meal?"

Bobo just looked at the old man and said nothing.

"Bobo, he is talking to you. Answer him," said Zvina.

"Yes," replied Bobo, looking at the old man.

"Do you like toys? Do you have…"

"Yes, he does. He always takes my toys!" Fari interrupted the old man.

"Is that right? You are the big brother. Big brothers let their younger brothers play with their toys," said the old man.

"But he breaks them."

"That's alright. Mum and Dad always buy new ones, right?" said the old man, pointing at Jill and Zvina.

"Mum and Dad don't always have the money to buy new toys," said Jill, laughing.

"Ok. What's your name?" the old man asked Bobo.

"My name is Bobo."

"What a nice name. Do you have a teddy bear at home?"

"Yes. I have one."

"Ok. Here is another one. Now you have two," said the old man, giving Bobo a small, brown teddy bear. It looked more like a puppy than a bear. Bobo was a little surprised at the gift from the stranger. He looked at the old man for a moment, and then turned to look at his parents, silently asking for their approval to accept the gift.

"You may have it, Bobo," said Jill, smiling at the old man.

"Thank you," said Bobo with a grin as he received the teddy.

"Bye, now. See you next time, and have fun with your teddies," said the old man as he walked away.

"Thank you very much," Jill and Zvina said at the same time.

After the old man left, Jill turned to Zvina and said, "He is such a generous old man. I wonder why such an old man would have bought a teddy bear, just to give it away to a stranger."

"Maybe he won it in some form of competition and he doesn't have any grandchildren to give it to," suggested Zvina.

After finishing their breakfast, the family got into the car and started their journey to Grand Forks. As they drove out of the city, they came to an intersection controlled by traffic lights. While waiting at the intersection, they were rear-ended by a young woman driving a smaller car. Luckily, the impact was not very hard, and no one got injured. Their vehicle did not get badly damaged either. The young woman appeared to be intoxicated, so Zvina called the police to the scene. After giving the police a statement of what had happened, Zvina and his family proceeded on their journey.

"Bobo! Are you going to give your teddy a name?"

"Yes. His name is Doggy," replied Bobo. "I like him."

"Good for you," said Jill as she turned around to look at Bobo who was sitting in the back seat.

"Hey, honey! Time flies. Who would have seen this coming? A few hours from now we will be citizens of

Canada. Remember what we went through to get permanent residency?"

"Yes. It has been quite a journey. It's something I always want to forget because it was such a painful experience, but you know what? This story needs to be told to our grandkids and all our descendants for generations to come. It's a valuable part of our family history. Our descendants will need to know how we came to Canada," said Zvina.

"You are right," agreed Jill.

"I think I should write a book. That way I can guarantee the story will not get distorted as it gets passed down from generation to generation."

"That's a good idea. We have come a long way. The other thing, honey, is that we have lived in three different cities since we landed. I hope we are not going to move again soon."

"Are you tired of following me in my elusive dreams?"

"Hahaha!" laughed Jill. "You remind me of that song by Cocoa T that you used to play when we were at university."

Zvina started singing the song and Jill joined in.

You followed me to Sheffield
You followed me to Castleford
We didn't find it there
So we moved on
You went with me to Vancouver
Things looked good in Trail
We didn't find it there
So we moved on
I know you are tired of following my elusive dreams
and schemes
For they are only fleeting things
My elusive dreams

It was fun driving on the highway singing that song on this day when they were finally getting their Canadian citizenship. They were very excited.

They arrived at the Grand Forks Community Hall half an hour before the ceremony started. They joined the queue at the registration desk to present their notices to appear and other requested documentation. After registration, they went inside the hall and took their seats in the reserved section with the other citizenship candidates. Within a few moments, the platform party entered the hall and the presiding judge took the stand. He welcomed everyone and gave a brief speech about the importance of this day to the citizenship candidates and their families. The presiding judge then asked the candidates to raise their right hands and he led the oath in both English and French.

I swear that I will be faithful
And bear true allegiance
To Her Majesty Queen Elizabeth the Second
Queen of Canada
Her Heirs and Successors
And that I will faithfully observe
The laws of Canada
And fulfil my duties
As a Canadian citizen.

After taking the oath, the candidates sat down and the clerk called each candidate forward to receive their citizenship certificates. When all the candidates had taken their seats, the presiding judge congratulated the candidates and welcomed them into Canada's family. He then asked everybody to stand up and sing Canada's National Anthem. This marked the end of the ceremony.

"Hurrah! We are Canadian citizens!" shouted Zvina as he joined his wife and kids in a group hug.

"We should have some photos taken with the presiding judge and other special guests," Jill suggested.

"Yes," replied Zvina, "and the other new citizens as well. We should have photos with the South African couple from Trail."

After taking the photos, Zvina and his family joined their fellow new citizens, guests, and officials in the after–ceremony reception.

Chapter Two

Making the Decision – Year 2000

When Zvina finished work, he went to join his three friends who were already carousing at their usual pub in the city centre. After struggling to find parking, he finally spotted two street kids waving at him to come to a parking spot where they were standing. Zvina pulled into the parking spot and got out of the car.

"Good evening, Sir," one of the street kids greeted him. "We will look after your car, Sir. Enjoy yourself, Sir. You know us; your car is safe. By the way, one of your friends just arrived too. His car is parked over there," said the street kid, pointing to Zvina's friend's car.

"Ok, young man," Zvina replied. "See you later."

Zvina locked his car and went into the pub. He spotted his three friends sitting in their usual corner. Zvina and his friends were very close. All four were best friends with each other. Zvina, an engineer at one of the biggest mining companies in Zimbabwe, worked for the same company as Muko, who was also an engineer. The other two friends were

Munya and Tindo. Munya was an engineer working for an international oil company. Tindo worked for an international bank. As Zvina approached the table where his friends were seated, Muko shouted,

"What kept you in the office for so long?"

"A client came in just as I was about to leave, so I had to go back into the office to talk to him," Zvina replied, pulling a chair out to take a seat.

"Who was the client? What does he want? Gold elution and smelting?" Muko asked again.

"Actually, neither of those. He told me that he just retired from city council. He got a good retirement package and he used some of the money to buy gold claims. He wants to go and take some samples at his claims and have them analyzed."

"Does he have any experience in mining and mineral processing? Does he think he can just build a mine and a plant using data from those grab samples? I usually don't entertain such idiots. You are very patient," Muko commented, taking a sip of beer.

"Muko, your problem is that you think everyone out there is smart like you. No. There are some people who are smarter than you in other walks of life. We cannot all be mining and mineral processing graduates," Munya intervened.

"Guys, the brother is thirsty; ask the waiter to bring him a beer," Tindo interjected. "I hope finding a parking spot wasn't that difficult for you," he continued, patting Zvina on the back.

"Not at all. Those street kids, your friends, found it for me," replied Zvina.

"But you know what? They are not actually street kids. I asked one of them and he told me that he lives in Mabvuku.

I thought he was lying, but I met him at a local bottle store in Mabvuku last weekend. I bought him a drink," said Tindo.

"Here you are, Sir," said the waiter as he passed a bottle of Castle Lager to Zvina. He went on to say, "When I saw Tindo sitting in the corner, I knew the whole crew was going to be here tonight. I am at your service. Enjoy yourselves, guys."

"By the way, we are going to Mereki's tomorrow. I need to fuel up my car. I can't make it there and back with less than a quarter tank. It's almost thirty kilometres from Mabvuku to Mereki. I am on a quarter tank right now," said Tindo.

Tindo lived in the suburb of Mabvuku, east of the city centre; and Munya and Zvina lived in Marlborough suburb, northwest of the city centre. Muko lived in Avondale, which was also northwest of the city centre but closer to the city centre than Marlborough.

"Where are you going to buy the fuel?" asked Muko.

"There are quite a number of gas stations along Mutare Road. There must be a few that have fuel. If I can't get fuel on my way home, then one of you guys must buy some fuel for me tomorrow morning and bring it over to my place," said Tindo, pointing at his friends.

"You are right," said Zvina sarcastically. "Who do you think is going to spend three hours in a queue to buy fuel for you?"

"Do you guys want me to leave now and go look for fuel?" asked Tindo.

"Don't worry, Tindo. There have been a few deliveries this week and many gas stations have fuel. You will get fuel on your way home," Munya reassured Tindo.

"Guys, on a serious note, this fuel shortage is driving me crazy. Do you think it's going to end soon, or is it going to get worse?" Muko asked his friends. He frowned before taking a big gulp of beer.

"It's going to end soon, I think. We have big international oil companies here. They just need time to adjust to the business environment and their logistics will improve," answered Munya reassuringly.

"I hope that happens soon. I was very disappointed last weekend. I could not deliver bullbars to my client in Gweru because I couldn't get fuel. That's lost revenue for me, because bullbars are in great demand in Gweru and I am the only supplier. I also cancelled my trip to Machipanda the other weekend because I did not have fuel. We cannot continue like this," said Zvina, shaking his head.

"What did you want in Machipanda? There is nothing there," asked Tindo with a funny grin that showed his large incisors.

"My uncle is manufacturing freezits. I want to take a truckload and sell them there. Freezits sell pretty fast there, especially this time of the year," replied Zvina.

"Mr. Entrepreneur!!!!" shouted Muko, pointing at Zvina. "Don't waste your time doing that kind of stuff. Let's find out how we can get land. Zanu-PF is giving people land. We must join the bandwagon. Farming and mining are the only ways one can make money in this country. Money is in the soil, my friends."

"You are right, Muko," said Munya, "but we don't know anyone up there in Zanu-PF. Besides, the whole land distribution process is chaotic."

"Clever people shine in chaotic situations like this," said Muko, laughing and patting Munya on the back. "While everyone else is focusing on the pressing issues of the moment, clever people focus on making money."

"But how do you make money in this chaotic situation?" a puzzled Munya asked.

"By focusing on money," said Muko, showing his friends a bundle of notes he had pulled out of his pocket. "I mean by focusing on acquiring as much land as you can. By the time the chaos is over, you will have acquired thousands of hectares which you can keep, or sell, or even lease, and…"

"Guys, don't you have better things to talk about?" Tindo interjected. "We are just a bunch of little fish. Let the big fish in Zanu do their thing. The problem with Zanu–PF is that the former freedom fighters do not want to get out of power. They will not give youngsters like us a chance. It makes me sick. Please, let's talk about other things."

"Ok. Let's talk about soccer. At which pub are we going to watch the African Nations Cup qualifier match between Cameroon and Togo? I prefer Bulldog's Pub in Westgate. It doesn't get very full and the crowd there is less rowdy," said Munya.

"It's closer to home for all of us except Tindo," added Zvina. Turning to Tindo, he said, "You should move to the northwest of the city, my friend. Join the club." Zvina patted Tindo on the back.

Though they tried to veer away from discussing the tense political and economic situation in Zimbabwe, they kept coming back to it. When all was said and done, they agreed that things were not good in Zimbabwe. Even though they had each been working for over four years after graduating from The University of Zimbabwe, none of them could afford a house. It was the year 2000, twenty years after independence, but there was still no evidence of significant economic growth in the country. In fact, over the last few years the economy had declined. The rate of inflation was more than fifty percent. An economic meltdown was imminent.

After three hours of drinking and discussing various issues ranging from sports to business opportunities, the friends called it a day, paid their bill, and left the pub.

As Zvina approached his car, the young kid that had been looking after his car came running to him.

"Your car was in safe hands, Sir. Did you have a good time?" asked the kid.

"Of course, young man," answered Zvina, as he handed the kid three ten-dollar bills.

"Thank you, Sir. See you next time," said the kid, as he put the bills into his pocket.

Zvina got into his car and drove off behind his friends Munya and Muko.

Two weeks later, Zvina and Muko were in their office working when Zvina's phone rang.

"What's happening, Munya?" Zvina answered the phone.

"Where are you guys going for lunch?" asked Munya from the other end of the line.

"We haven't decided yet. Do you have a place in mind?" asked Zvina.

"Tell him that we are going to Mai George's place in Mbare," shouted Muko.

"Muko says Mai George's in Mbare is good. Does that work for you?" Zvina asked Munya.

"Sure. That works. I will call Tindo and let him know. What time should we meet there?"

"Twelve forty-five should be good. What do you think, Muko?" asked Zvina.

Muko nodded in agreement.

"Ok. Twelve forty-five it is. See you there," replied Munya from the other end of the line.

At lunch time Zvina and Muko got into Muko's car and drove off to Mai George's place in Mbare. When they arrived, they had to park quite some distance from the house because the whole street was full of cars. Mai George's place had become a very popular place in Harare. Although it was located in Mbare, the oldest, most crowded, and most notorious high-density suburb in the city, it surprisingly attracted clientele from elite places such as Borrowdale, Mt Pleasant, Avondale, and others. Drawing mostly professionals in their early twenties to middle age, it was a place where one would meet old friends from university, college, or even high school. About ninety-five percent of Mai George's patrons were male. Mai George had turned her house into a restaurant. She had built a big shack in the backyard, which served as an eating area. Next to that shack was another shack which she used as the kitchen. The kitchen was filled with smoke from the wood stoves that were located in the middle. The chefs in the kitchen were three big, fat ladies and one man. The man could be seen making sadza *(maize meal)* most of the time, while the three women each had her own pot of beef bones, beef stew, pork bones, chicken stew, beef tripe, or beef intestines. Just outside the kitchen shack two women dished out food from big pots. There was one toilet at the far end of the backyard with a tap and a concrete sink just outside. This was where people washed their hands. The place was infested with houseflies all year round and the sanitary conditions were appalling. Any health inspector in their right senses would have shut this place down the moment they saw it. Yet the place continued to get more popular.

A number of places had sprouted throughout the city that offered similar services, but most of them were located on licensed business premises. Mai George's place was not licensed, and it was like a disaster waiting to happen. Given its popularity a lot of people wondered why the authorities were not shutting it down. Another puzzling aspect of Mai George's place was that the patrons were mostly middle class. One would expect to see them in restaurants downtown or in the eastern or northern suburbs, but Mai George had defied the odds.

"How much do you charge for looking after my car while I have lunch at Mai George's?" Muko asked a street kid after pulling into a parking spot.

"Whatever you can afford, brother. Your younger brother is hungry. He needs something just to buy him a meal," replied the kid.

"I will see how much I have left in change from Mai George's. Ok?"

"Sure, brother. I will be here."

"You gotta love Mbare," said Zvina, as they walked towards Mai George's place. "I hope Munya and Tindo are here. I don't see Munya's car on this side."

"Maybe he parked on the other side," suggested Muko.

"Hey! We are over here," shouted Tindo, waving at Zvina and Muko. Tindo and Munya were already in the queue to buy food.

Zvina and Muko joined Tindo and Munya in the queue. They waited in the queue for about fifteen minutes before buying their food, and then they sat in the big shack in the backyard. By the time they finished their lunch, the place was so full that some patrons could not find seats. They had to eat their food while standing outside.

"This is one of the dirtiest places I have ever eaten at, but I still like it," said Muko, as he slurped up soup from his plate.

"Have you ever wondered why we like this place?" asked Munya.

"We like this place because we are also dirty," said Tindo, laughing.

"I think it brings out the African in us. The way the food is cooked, the way it is served, and the environment we eat it in are just like how they do it at traditional ceremonies in the rural areas," answered Zvina. "I like it."

"What's missing here is beer. She should start selling beer," Munya suggested.

"As it is right now, this is an illegal operation, but because it is quite peaceful here, she gets away with it. I think if she starts selling beer, they will shut her down because drunkards will always cause trouble and police will get involved. Also, Mbare thieves will swarm this place because it's easier to steal from drunk people. That will drive away her customers. I think she knows this, and that's why she intends to keep it the way it is. That's why she doesn't operate in the evenings," Muko said as he stood up. "Let's go, guys. Give the seats to other patrons."

They all stood up and went over to the sink to wash their hands. After washing their hands, Tindo bought soft drinks which they drank while standing next to the toilet in the backyard. After finishing the soft drinks, they handed back the empty bottles, went back to their cars, and returned to work.

Later that afternoon, as usual, Zvina went to the gym. Although Zvina and his wife Jill, a pharmacist, had both been working for several years, the couple could not afford a house in the low-density suburbs of Harare. They were renting a cottage in Marlborough. However, they had recently bought a lot in Marlborough which they were hoping to develop in the near future. On his way home Zvina passed through Westgate Mall to pick up his wife from the pharmacy where she worked. At the mall, the couple bought a few groceries and then they went home. When they arrived at home, their one-year-old son came out to meet them with the maid following closely behind him. Jill got out of the car and handed the grocery bags to the maid before picking up Fari. As Zvina got out of the car, his cellphone rang.

"Hello there, Zvina speaking," he answered.

"Hi Zvina," said the caller, "I am calling to let you know that we have run out of bullbars and we have some orders which are wanted ASAP. Can you bring bullbars to Gweru this weekend? If you can bring ten bullbars and five tail bars, that should be fine for the next two to three weeks."

"This is very short notice. I hope my supplier will have some on hand. I will call you back tomorrow to confirm once I talk to my supplier. Ok?" said Zvina, as he entered the house.

"That's fine. Talk to you tomorrow then. Bye now," said the caller before hanging up.

Besides working full time as an engineer, Zvina also ran a small business on the side through which he bought and sold bullbars. In Gweru, he had partnered with a car dealer who sold and installed the bullbars. Sales in Gweru had been very good and were growing such that every two to three weeks Zvina had to deliver more than a dozen bullbars and tail bars. Zvina delivered the bullbars himself in his half-tonne truck because it was cheaper.

"Hi, Fari. What's up, Mister? How was your day?" Zvina asked his son as he took him from Jill.

"How was your day, Daddy?" the maid asked Zvina as she knelt down next to the coffee table in the living room.

"My day was good, Sisy. Thank you," answered Zvina, sitting on the sofa with his son on his lap.

The maid stood up and left the living room.

"Mai Fari," Zvina said to his wife, "I might go to Gweru this Saturday morning. They have run out of bullbars there, so I have to bring them some more. Chipo just called me as I was getting out of the car."

"Do you think your supplier will have enough manufactured bullbars in stock by Saturday morning?" asked Jill.

"Well, he will have to do something for me. I will call him first thing tomorrow morning," replied Zvina.

"Are you going to come back on Saturday, or do you plan to spend the night in Gweru?" Jill asked again.

"I want to come back on the same day," replied Zvina.

"Ok. That's fine. This bullbar business is doing pretty good. Keep it up. It should help us raise money to build our own house on the lot. I am sick and tired of living in a cottage," said Jill.

"I hope I won't have trouble finding fuel. In fact, I think I should fill up my jerrycan here in Harare in case there is no fuel in Gweru or in other towns along the way. Remember how last time I had to ask Muko to bring me fuel in Chegutu when I ran out of fuel there? I am not taking any chances this time."

The maid walked in and asked, "Shall I serve you dinner now?"

"Sure. Go ahead," Jill answered.

The maid went back into the kitchen and returned with three bowls of food, which she placed on the coffee table. Their dinner was the typical staple maize meal (sadza) served with oxtail stew and fried kale. This was Zvina's favourite meal. He had to have this meal at least twice a week.

The following morning, Zvina called his bullbar supplier, who confirmed that he would have his order ready for pickup by the end of the day. After work Zvina went to pick up the bullbars from his supplier at Machipisa Home Industries. His next task was to fuel up his truck and the jerrycan. After a couple of hours of driving around town looking for a fuel station with diesel, he came across a long queue and he joined it. It took him another two hours before he was served.

"Can you fill up my jerrycan too, please?" Zvina asked the attendant after he had finished filling the truck.

"No, Sir. I can't. I am not allowed to put fuel in jerrycans or drums," replied the attendant.

Zvina moved closer to the attendant, pulled out a bunch of notes, and gave them to the attendant. Zvina whispered, "That's yours, my man. Please, I need the jerrycan filled as well."

Without a word, the attendant accepted the notes and filled up Zvina's jerrycan. Zvina paid for the diesel and pulled off.

"This is ridiculous," Zvina thought to himself. "How long are we going to be looking for fuel around town like this? That's four hours of my time gone for nothing. I should have used this time doing something more productive. I can't stand this. Anyway, let me find out where the boys are. If they are in Bulldog's Pub I will pass through and have a few quick beers. I have to go to sleep early because I want to leave for Gweru by six in the morning."

Zvina pulled over to the side of the road and called Muko.

"Hey, Chief! Where are you?" Zvina asked Muko.

"I am in Bulldog's Pub with Munya," Muko replied. "Where are you?"

"I have been looking for fuel for the past four hours. I finally got it and I am on my way home. I will pass through there in a few minutes. See you," said Zvina.

When Zvina arrived at Westgate Mall he parked his truck near the entrance to the parking lot and went over to see the guard in the entrance guardroom.

"Hello, Officer," he greeted the guard. "How are you today?"

"I am fine, Sir. How can I help you today?" asked the guard.

"Could you kindly keep an eye on my truck? I have got bullbars in the truck and they are unsecured. I will give you some change for a drink when I come back," Zvina asked the guard, as he leaned over the guardroom window.

"No problem, my friend. That's why I am here," replied the guard.

"Thank you, Officer. See you later," said Zvina, as he walked towards the entrance to the mall.

When Zvina entered Bulldog's Pub he spotted his three friends sitting by the bar counter talking to the bartender.

"Look who's here!" shouted Mucha, pointing at Zvina. "That was quick. Where were you when you called Muko?" asked Mucha.

Mucha was another member of Zvina's group of friends, although he was somewhat of an outsider. He did not hang out with the group very often. He was an accountant working for the same company as Muko and Zvina.

"I wasn't very far. What's up, boys?" said Zvina, greeting Muko and Munya.

"Give him a very cold beer, Mdakwisi (bartender)," Muko asked the bartender. "He has been in a queue for diesel for four hours. He must be very thirsty, hungry, and angry," Muko continued as he laughed at Zvina.

"I think he needs some chicken wings too," said Munya, laughing.

"You guys think this is a laughing matter. I am really frustrated by this," Zvina said, picking up the beer bottle the bartender had placed on the counter.

"Were you totally out of diesel? You could have waited for tomorrow. It's easier to find gas on Saturdays than Fridays when everybody is filling up to go out of town for the weekend," Mucha said.

"You are right, but that's not until Saturday afternoon. I want to leave town at six a.m. tomorrow. I am delivering bullbars to Gweru," replied Zvina.

"There goes Mr. Businessman," said Munya, laughing. "But on a serious note, how are you doing? Are you making any profit? We might be witnessing the birth of a large business corporation here," Munya continued rather sarcastically.

"If you see me putting my time into it like this, it means I am getting something out of it. It might not be much, but it's worth it," replied Zvina.

"Good for you," said Munya.

"Hey Munya, let the brother do what he has to do. In this country, going into business is the way to go. Our problem is that we have been raised with the mentality that we have to be employed by some big company. That should be a thing of the past. If we need to control the economy of this country, we need to own businesses. Otherwise, the white men will continue to control the economy," Muko said in a very assertive voice, clenching his right hand into a fist.

"There you go again. You have to turn every subject or issue into a discussion about politics," Munya interjected.

The friends continued talking while enjoying beer and chicken wings well into the evening. When Zvina checked his watch, it was almost ten p.m.

"Guys, I have to go now. I have to be up early, like I said," Zvina said as he took the last sip from his glass of beer.

"Hey, hey boy! Take it easy. Have one for the road. Mdakwisi, give him the last one," said Muko, trying to convince Zvina to stay a little longer.

"Ok. I will have the last one," said Zvina, accepting another beer from the bartender.

He quickly drank the beer, placed a bunch of notes on the counter, bade his friends farewell, and left the pub. In the parking lot, he passed by the guardroom and gave the guard some money for looking after his truck. When he got home, his wife was still awake watching TV with the maid and his nephew Simo. Simo had recently come from Bocha, the home of Zvina's tribal rural roots. He was living with them and studying at Harare Polytechnic.

Zvina greeted everybody before sitting down on the sofa next to his wife.

"I thought you would be home early today since you are driving to Gweru very early in the morning. You need to get enough rest. It's going to be a long day for you driving all the way to Gweru and back," said Jill, looking at her husband.

"You are right. I would have been home a couple of hours ago, but after spending two hours looking for a gas station with fuel and another two hours waiting in a queue to fuel up, I got so frustrated and stressed out that I had to relieve myself of that stress by having a few beers at the pub," replied Zvina.

"That's not a very good excuse. Sisy, please give him his supper. He has to go to bed right away," Jill asked the maid.

Immediately after his supper, Zvina went to bed.

The following morning Zvina left the house at six o'clock. Since it was a Saturday morning, the highway was not very busy. By nine a.m. he was in Gweru. He went to the car dealership and dropped off the bullbars. He had a long meeting with the car dealership manager in which they discussed exploring other markets in smaller towns near Gweru. They also discussed exploring the mining and the agriculture markets in that province. These industries had huge potential.

After the meeting, Zvina left the dealership and went to meet his friend at a local bottle store which they had often frequented together when Zvina lived in Gweru. His friend was there already, drinking beer and barbequing. By the time they had finished their barbeque, it was already mid-afternoon.

"Kiri, I have to go now," Zvina said to his friend. "I don't want to drive after sunset. Besides, if I stay longer, we will only keep drinking. I can't get on the highway drunk."

"You are right. After a few weeks of not seeing each other I would be tempted to persuade you to stay a couple more hours, but it's not safe," agreed Kiri.

Zvina bade Kiri farewell and left for Harare.

Three weeks had passed since Zvina had delivered his shipment of bullbars to Gweru. His business partner was expecting Zvina to bring another shipment to Gweru, but the fuel shortage had interfered with these plans.

One evening, as Zvina drove to Westgate Mall to meet his friends at Bulldog's Pub, he started thinking about the latest economic developments in the country and how they were affecting him.

"The fuel situation is really getting out of hand. One day, when the country completely runs out of fuel, we will be forced to park our cars. I was supposed to deliver freezits to sell in Machipanda tomorrow, but because I could not find fuel, I have had to cancel the trip. This is ridiculous. That's a lost business opportunity. The freezits order is a big order. God knows when I will get the fuel to deliver this order. If the truck was not loaded with freezits, half a tank could take me across the border. Once I cross the border I would be fine because there is plenty of fuel in Mozambique. But of course, the truck is loaded with freezits, and so I do not have enough fuel to even make it to Mutare which is ten kilometres from the boarder. I have just half a tank now and the whole city is literally dry. Should I just take my chances and go tomorrow morning? The problem is by the time I leave the city, I will have less than half a tank. I don't want to be stuck on the highway when I run out of fuel."

As Zvina pulled into a parking spot at Westgate Mall he was still lost in thought. He parked his truck and went into Bulldog's Pub. In the pub, Tindo and Muko were sitting in their usual spot by the bar counter. Zvina greeted his friends, pulled out a stool, and sat down next to Muko.

"Mdakwisi," Muko called the bartender, "here is another thirsty one. You know what he drinks."

"Sure. I know he drinks Castle Lager," the bartender replied. He proceeded to open a cold bottle of Castle Lager and handed it over to Zvina.

"Are you still going to Machipanda tomorrow?" Tindo asked Zvina. "If you are, I could come with you. I am off tomorrow."

"No. I could not get fuel. The city is literally dry. I made some calls around town this afternoon and none of the gas stations I called had gas," Zvina replied.

"What do you want to do in Machipanda?" Muko asked.

"I wanted to deliver freezits. I got an order from this guy who owns a grocery store there. It's a big order. Five thousand freezits," replied Zvina.

"You and your business ideas," said Muko, patting Zvina on his back. "You are really serious about this. I think it's time we take you seriously and join you."

"Well, it would be good to team up and do bigger stuff. But the fuel shortage problem is hampering everything. You can't do anything without fuel. If I can't deliver this freezits order, just imagine how much money I will have lost. It pisses me off," said Zvina, shaking his head.

"You are right," said Tindo. "And you know what? It's going to get worse. I think one of these days we will have to park our cars and ride bicycles. Just mark my words," Tindo laughed.

"I totally agree with you, Tindo," said Zvina. "I can't help but wonder why we should stick around and die in this mess. I sometimes think about going down South (South Africa). Farai seems to be doing pretty well down there. When he came for Christmas he was driving the latest BMW 3 series. He said I could stay with him until I find a job."

"Why don't you take him up on his offer?" asked Tindo.

"My wife does not want to live in South Africa. She says there is a lot of crime down there," replied Zvina.

"There is crime in every country. You just have to avoid places with high crime rates. It's like here in Harare. There are some parts of Harare that you just don't go," remarked Muko.

"I know. But I just couldn't convince my wife. I gave up," said Zvina.

"I have never liked the idea of living in South Africa. If I have to leave this country, I will go to either Canada or Australia. They have good immigration programs for professionals, but the application process can take very long," said Muko.

"Speaking of Canada, I have an uncle there. You remember my uncle who used to live in the UK? He married a Canadian and moved to Canada. I don't know if I would like to live in Canada. They say winters there are very long and extremely cold. Australia would be better," said Zvina.

"Something to think about. I have been to Canada. I attended a conference in Edmonton, Alberta when I was doing my PhD. While I was there, I drove around Edmonton and I saw and learned quite a bit about it. I liked it. We also drove to the Rocky Mountains. I liked the scenery," said Muko.

"I don't think I will leave this country. I think things will get worse, but I also think that at some point things will get back to normal," said Tindo.

"You don't know when things will get better," said Muko. "I would rather go now and come back when things get better. I have accepted a job in Mexico on a two-year work permit. In the meantime, I am going to apply for Canadian permanent residency. When my work permit in Mexico expires, I want to go to Canada if things are still bad here."

"When is your permit coming out?" asked Tindo.

"Anytime now. I am supposed to start at the new job in six weeks," replied Muko.

"Ohh! Here comes the tall one," said Zvina, looking at Munya who had just entered the pub.

"What's up boys?" said Munya.

"Mdakwisi! Another thirsty one." As usual, Muko called the bartender.

"Munya, you are the oil guy. Where can I find diesel in the city today or tomorrow morning?" Zvina asked Munya.

"There is no fuel in town, my friend. Nothing! Zero! Our tanks are empty and we are not expecting any deliveries this weekend. I am told the vessel with our next delivery docks in Beira in four days' time. Conserve whatever you have now or you may have to park your vehicle for a couple of days or so," advised Munya.

The four men continued to drink beer and talk about the fuel shortage issue well into the evening. Occasionally, other people in the pub joined the dialogue. From the conversations, it was evident that Zimbabwe was in crisis. The fuel shortage was affecting all sectors of the economy. The already fragile economy, which had been battered by bad political decisions and corruption, was on the verge of a sudden collapse. Skilled workers, especially those in engineering and medical professions, were trickling out of the country because of the economic crisis caused by the fuel shortage. Headhunters and immigration lawyers from developed countries with skilled labour shortages like Australia, Canada, and UK had descended on the country because they knew it would be easy to recruit professionals who were frustrated by the economic situation in Zimbabwe. They were holding recruitment seminars. They also ran advertisements with immigration information and employment opportunities in local newspapers. Zvina and his wife had already attended one seminar on emigrating to Australia. They had also responded to an advertisement about emigrating to Canada by requesting an information package. Although this seemed like a good move given the current situation in the country, the idea of living overseas, where there were no relatives and friends, was daunting to Zvina. But the worse things got, the more seriously Zvina entertained the idea of moving overseas.

Three months later, Zvina received the information package from a Canadian Immigration law firm. According to the package, the first step in the application process was to complete an assessment form which had a scoring system to determine your eligibility based on age, qualifications, work experience, etc. Zvina and Jill completed the assessment form. They had each scored very high, which meant that their chances of getting permanent residency in Canada were high. They started thinking seriously about emigrating to Canada. They consulted with most of their friends and relatives on the issue. Most of them liked the idea, and they encouraged Zvina and Jill to make the move. Muko had already left for Mexico and he seemed to like it there. He had also submitted his application for Canadian permanent residency and he had told Zvina that it was a simple process.

However, Zvina and Jill remained skeptical. After several days of pondering this decision, they decided that Zvina should visit Canada first. He could get firsthand information about life in Canada before they applied for permanent residency. He would visit his uncle who was living in Canada.

"I think that's the best we can do in this situation. I would hate to apply for permanent residency and move overseas, only to realize that I don't like the country for one reason or another," Zvina said to his wife while they were sitting on their cottage veranda one Saturday afternoon.

"You are right. I think you should call Uncle Loxi and ask him if he is ok with you visiting him for a month," Jill replied.

"Sure. I have his phone number, but I can't call him using my cellphone. It's very expensive. I have to find someone who will let me use their landline and then I will pay them for that call when they get their bill at the end of the month," said Zvina.

"Munya has a landline. Why don't you ask him?" suggested Jill.

"That's right. You know what? I will call him right now, and if he is home, I will go and make the call right away. It must be in the morning in Canada. It's the right time to call Uncle Loxi," said Zvina, as he pulled out his cellphone to call Munya.

"Hi, Munya. I need you to do me a big favour," said Zvina, standing up and walking towards his truck.

"Anything for you, brother. What can I do for you?" asked Munya from the other end of the line.

"I need to call my uncle Loxi in Canada, but it's very expensive using the cellphone. Can I use your landline? I will pay for that call when you get your bill," said Zvina.

"No problem. When do you want to make the call?" asked Munya.

"Are you home right now? I could swing by now," asked Zvina.

"Yes, I am home. Come over and bring a six pack of Castle Lager. I am thirsty," said Munya, laughing.

"Ok. See you in a few minutes," said Zvina jumping into his truck. He called out the window to his wife, "Honey, I will see you later. Munya says I can call Uncle Loxi from his landline. I will pass through the mall on my way back. Do you want me to get anything for you?"

"No. Don't worry. We are ok here," replied Jill.

Zvina waved at his son who was sitting on his mum's lap and drove away. When he arrived at Munya's place, he did not waste time. He asked for the phone, so he could make the call.

"Hello, who is this?" came the voice from the other end of the line.

"Hi, Uncle. It's Zvina. Are you still sleeping? You sound tired and sleepy," Zvina asked his uncle.

"Ahh, Zvina. It's you? Yah, I came home very late. I was at the pub with my friends. How are you?" said Loxi.

"I am fine. Is it a good time to talk? I could call in a few hours when you are up," offered Zvina.

"Yes, it's ok. I am good. How is everyone in Zimbabwe? How is Gogo (Loxi's mum)?" asked Loxi.

"Everyone is fine. It's been a long time since you were here. Everyone misses you. When are you coming to Zimbabwe?" asked Zvina.

"I am not sure. I am trying to set up a small fashion store here with one of my friends. I am the one who runs the store, so I can't go on holiday until the store is well-established to the point where I can afford to hire employees," replied Loxi.

"Ok. Uncle, as you know, this is a very expensive call. Let me get straight to my reason for calling. Things in this country are deteriorating more each day. The economy is almost on its knees and there are no signs of things improving in the near future. The political situation is even worse. I would not be surprised if we have a civil war in the next few months. Just to give you the flavour of things here, on the economy side of things, we have not had any fuel supplies into the country for more than a week. So, everything is at a standstill. On the political front, the Commercial Farmers' Union and the government failed to reach an agreement on land redistribution. As a result, liberation war veterans are leading a campaign to invade commercial farms and take the land from white farmers. It's…"

"Are things that bad? Oh my God. I had no idea," Loxi interjected.

"Yes. The situation here is deteriorating pretty fast. Anyway, my wife and I have decided that we should leave this country ASAP," said Zvina.

"So where do you want to go? You should come to Canada," suggested Loxi.

"There you go. That's why I called you. We have heard that Canada is a very good country, but before we make the decision to emigrate there, I want to come over and see for myself. Could I come to stay with you for a month so I can find out more about Canada before I make a decision?" asked Zvina.

"No problem at all. As a matter of fact, I wish you could just come for good. We can deal with the paperwork while you are here. I know you will like it. I can't wait to have you here," said Loxi.

"That's good to know. Thank you," said Zvina.

"When do you want to come?" asked Loxi.

"I am not sure yet, but definitely in the next two to three months. I will let you know in about two weeks," replied Zvina.

"No problem. Like I said, I am running the store by myself, so I will not be going anywhere this summer. So whatever time works for you, I am ok with that," said Loxi.

"By the way, you live in Alberta, right?" asked Zvina.

"Yes. Calgary is the name of the city," replied Loxi.

"Ok, Uncle. I will call you in two weeks once I have firm plans. I have to let you go," said Zvina.

"Ok. Pass on my regards to everyone in the family. Take care. Bye now," said Loxi.

"Bye, Uncle. Speak to you soon," said Zvina, hanging up the phone.

"Man, you are serious about going to Canada," Munya said, passing his friend a bottle of Castle Lager.

"I am serious, man. I want to go and see how it is in person before I apply for permanent residency," said Zvina.

"That's a good idea. When are you leaving?" asked Munya.

"I haven't finalized the dates yet, but it should be in the next two to three months," replied Zvina.

After drinking a couple of beers each, Zvina and Munya got into Zvina's truck and went to meet their friends at Bulldog's Pub at the mall. However, before they got to the mall, Tindo called and asked them to join him at Mereki for barbeque. They would go to Bulldog's Pub after the barbeque.

Chapter Three

Preparations

When Zvina entered his manager's office, Mr. Smith lifted up his head and asked, "What brings you into my office first thing in the morning? Did you have a good weekend?"

"Sure, Sir. How about you?" replied Zvina.

"My weekend was good. Take a seat," said Mr. Smith, pointing to a chair in front of his desk.

"Did you play golf this weekend?" asked Zvina politely as he sat down.

"Yes, I played on Saturday. It was a good game but it was very hot," replied Mr. Smith.

Zvina and Mr. Smith had a very good working relationship. Mr. Smith had recruited Zvina from another division of their organization almost a year ago. The move was very good for Zvina because it had enabled him to relocate to Harare where his wife worked. Also, most of his relatives lived in Harare. As Zvina pondered about how to break the ice, he felt guilty. When Mr. Smith was recruiting him, Zvina had promised him a four-year commitment in the role. He knew that Mr. Smith would be disappointed that he was leaving the organization. Also, this was the first time in his career that Zvina had to resign from an organization. As he sat facing Mr. Smith, Zvina could feel beads of sweat forming on his forehead.

"Well, what can I do for you, young man?" asked Mr. Smith.

"I have something very important I want to discuss with you. May I close the door?" asked Zvina.

"Sure. Go ahead," replied Mr. Smith.

Zvina stood up and closed the door.

"Well, Sir," Zvina began, "as you are aware, things are getting worse every day in this country. The economy is crumbling and the political situation is a total mess."

"You are right, Zvina. The situation is getting out of hand. I hope something happens soon before the economy collapses completely. If it gets worse than this, the damage will be difficult to repair. It will take decades to get back to where we were," interjected Mr. Smith.

"For sure. As a result, I have decided to join other professionals that are leaving the country for greener pastures overseas," said Zvina.

"Really?" exclaimed Mr. Smith. "I am not very pleased to hear this, but I don't blame you. Young people like you have a long career ahead of you. You can't afford to languish in Zimbabwe when there are better opportunities elsewhere. You know, from the day Muko resigned, saying that he was leaving the country, I knew something like this would happen. You and Muko are such good friends, and I could see you joining him wherever he was going. Are you going to the same country as him?"

"Well, eventually we will be in the same country," replied Zvina.

"What you mean 'eventually'?" asked Mr. Smith.

"Muko got a two-year work permit in Mexico. He will be there for the next two years. When his permit expires he wants to go to Canada. I am going straight to Canada," replied Zvina.

"I see. You know that Canadian winters are very cold and long?" asked Mr. Smith.

"Yes, I know. It's something I am going to have to get used to, I guess," replied Zvina.

"Why don't you try Australia? It is just as good as Canada. In fact, I think its mining industry is bigger than Canada's. There are more opportunities there and the weather is just perfect in most parts of the country," said Mr. Smith.

"I thought about that, but I do not want to emigrate to a country that I do not have firsthand information about. I would like to visit the country before making a decision. I would like to see and assess things for myself. I do not know anyone in Australia, so I can't go there for a visit. It would be very expensive to stay in a hotel while I find out about the country. I have an uncle in Canada, and I plan to visit him for a month or two. During that time I can gather information that will help me make an informed decision," explained Zvina.

"There is nothing I can do to keep you here. Good luck in your search for greener pastures. Please write a resignation letter and bring it to me. I will pass it on to HR. By the way, do you know that your notice period is one month?" said Mr. Smith.

"Yes, I do. I will write the resignation letter and bring it to you. Thank you," replied Zvina.

Mr. Smith looked up and was silent for a moment. He was thinking.

"What's on your mind, Sir?" asked Zvina.

"My advice to you is that you shouldn't resign. Just apply for a three-month leave-of-absence. If things don't go well for you, you can always come back to your job. If all goes well, you resign in absentia. Sometimes immigration officials in these first world countries give people a hard time if they cannot prove that they are employed in their home country. Unemployed people have no good reason to go back to their third world countries and usually end up living in these first world countries illegally. They can deny you entry if you cannot prove that you have a job in your home country. If you apply for a leave-of-absence, I will give you a letter of employment to take with you. That may help you if you get asked about employment. I am doing this to help you in your travels. I will be filling your position sometime in the near future, because I am assuming you are gone for good. If things don't work out for you and you must come back to Zimbabwe, and your position is filled at that time, consider yourself unemployed."

"I am ok with that, Sir. Thank you for the advice. I will do that."

Zvina stood up and left Mr. Smith's office. He was shocked by Mr. Smith's response. He had thought that Mr. Smith would not have taken his resignation so lightly. After all, Mr. Smith had specifically asked him to commit to four years in that position before he hired him, and he had agreed. He felt like he was betraying Mr. Smith. As Zvina walked back to his office, he wondered how Mr. Smith would treat him during his notice period. He had always enjoyed a very good relationship with Mr. Smith, but now he was worried that Mr. Smith would treat him differently since he had broken his promise. He went back into his office and typed the application letter for leave-of-absence. He printed it, signed it, and gave it to Mr. Smith.

"You have a car loan with the company, don't you?" asked Mr. Smith as he accepted Zvina's application letter for leave-of-absence.

"Yes, I do," replied Zvina.

"That money you owe becomes due immediately. How do you want to pay it?" asked Mr. Smith.

"I will be selling my truck. Once it is bought, I will pay up," replied Zvina.

"No problem. I will ask the accounting department to get in touch with you so you can make arrangements with them," said Mr. Smith.

"Ok. Thank you," replied Zvina.

"We are going to have to take you for a farewell lunch one of these days and then for a drink after work. I will let you know when," said Mr. Smith.

"Thank you. I'd really appreciate that," said Zvina.

"Ok, young man. I guess you have not told the technicians that you are leaving yet?" asked Mr. Smith.

"No, I haven't. That would have been very unprofessional. I had to tell you first," replied Zvina.

"No problem. You can go and tell them. They will be very disappointed. In the very short period that you have been here, you have made very good working relationships with them. They all like working with you. Go ahead. Go and tell them," said Mr. Smith.

"I have to go and tell Farai first before I tell them. He is my senior. He would be disappointed if he was the last person to know," said Zvina.

"You are right. He would be disappointed," said Mr. Smith.

Zvina turned around and went to Farai's office. When he entered the office, Farai was on the phone. He gestured at Zvina to take a seat.

"I won't be long," Farai whispered to Zvina.

Zvina and Farai had first met each other at university, when Zvina was in his first year and Farai was in his fourth year in the department of Metallurgical Engineering. Later, they had worked together at a ferrochrome smelter in Gweru before Farai was transferred to their current division. Farai had recommended Zvina when Mr. Smith was looking for someone to fill a vacant position. Farai and Zvina also shared a very good working relationship.

Zvina took a seat and waited for Farai to finish his telephone conversation.

"You finally made up your mind about leaving the country?" asked Farai, putting the phone down.

"Yes, brother. Like I told you before, I am going on a fact-finding mission. If I find that it's a good place to live, then I will apply for permanent residency," replied Zvina.

"By the way, which country are you going to? Canada or Australia?" asked Farai.

"I will try Canada first," replied Zvina.

"I hear a lot of good things about Canada, but the extremely cold winters scare me off," said Farai. "I have been thinking about Australia. The climate there is not very different from our climate here."

"You are right. However, it's going to be easier for me to start a life in Canada because I have an uncle there. I can stay with him until I find a job. Then I can bring my wife and kid," said Zvina.

"I don't know anyone in Australia. I am going to look for a job in Australia while I am still here in Zimbabwe. When you get a job in Australia or in Canada, while you are still here, you are safe. The company will help with processing the papers for you. They will pay for your flights and temporary accommodation for the first few months while you settle. It makes the process of emigrating much easier," said Farai.

"That's a good way of going about it. In my case, I can't wait to find a job. I have to leave this country ASAP."

After discussing immigration issues and employment opportunities overseas for some time, Zvina left Farai's office and went to the laboratory. He wanted to convey the news of his departure to the technicians by himself.

"Good morning, Mr. Madzi," Zvina greeted the laboratory supervisor as he walked into the laboratory.

"Good morning, Sir. How are you this morning?" replied Mr. Madzi.

"I am fine. Can I talk to you for a minute in your office?" asked Zvina.

"Sure, Sir. Is everything ok?" asked Mr. Madzi as they walked into his office.

"Yes, everything is ok," replied Zvina, closing the door behind him.

"That's good. Take a seat, Sir. How can I help you this morning? Or should I ask what I have done wrong?" said Mr. Madzi, laughing.

Zvina sat down facing Mr. Madzi, took a deep breath, and shook his head before saying anything.

"Well, well, Mr. Madzi," Zvina started after a long pause, "we have worked very well together for some time now and we have enjoyed working with each other. Unfortunately, everything comes to an end. I have submitted my leave-of-absence application letter today but the reality is that I am moving on. I will not be coming back."

"What's the matter, Sir? I thought you enjoyed working here. You have had good working relationships with everyone from Mr. Smith all the way down to the messenger," said a surprised Mr. Madzi.

"It's not this place. I could work here until I retire. The economic and political situation in Zimbabwe has made me decide to leave. I am going to look for greener pastures overseas. I am going to Canada," replied Zvina.

"You are right. Things have been very bad lately and they seem to be getting worse every day. Young educated people like you should not waste their time here. Even though it's sad to see you go, given the situation in the country right now, I think that you are making the right decision. That's my boy!" said Mr. Madzi, patting Zvina on the back.

"I have convinced myself that it's the right decision for me right now," said Zvina.

"Don't forget your old man when you start making money overseas," Mr. Madzi said, with a big smile on his face. "When is your last day here? We must celebrate the good times we have had here. We should have a farewell barbeque for you."

"Exactly four weeks from now. My notice period is one month," replied Zvina.

"Good. That gives us enough time to make arrangements for the barbeque. Now, let's go and tell my other colleagues in the lab about your departure," said Mr. Madzi, opening the door.

Later that day, Zvina went to join his friends at their usual pub downtown.

"Hi guys," Zvina greeted his friends, Tindo and Munya, who were seated in their usual place.

"What's going on, brother? You look tired," asked Tindo.

"Yes, I am tired. Mentally though, not physically," replied Zvina.

"What is it? Did you resign today?" asked Munya.

"Yes, I did. I had people in my office for the most part of the day. You can imagine. Everybody wanted to know why I am leaving and where I am going. At one point, I just felt like locking my door and not letting anyone in. It was crazy," said Zvina.

"I envy you, sonny boy. You have guts," remarked Tindo.

"I need a very cold beer. Did you order beer? I see your glass is also empty," asked Zvina.

"Yes, I did. It's coming," replied Munya.

"What was the general response to the news of your departure? I mean were all these people who came to your office saying you should stay, or were they saying that it was a good move?" Tindo asked, handing Zvina a glass of beer.

"Most people said that given the current situation in Zimbabwe, this is a good move. Guess what? I did not know Farai is also making plans to leave. He told me that he wants to go Down Under. He is looking for a job there right now," said Zvina, after taking a long gulp from his beer glass.

"Really? He doesn't look like a person who would think about leaving the country. I am surprised," said Munya.

"I was surprised too. He doesn't usually tell people what he is up to," commented Zvina.

"Have you decided your departure date yet?" asked Tindo.

"Not yet, but I should by the end of this week. By mid next week I should book the flights," replied Zvina.

"Good luck, sonny boy. You will be fine," said Tindo.

"Of course, I will be fine. The main issue here is that I am going to miss this," said Zvina, pointing at his friends.

"That's the big problem. I will miss *gochi–gochi kwaMereki* (barbequing at Mereki), playing social soccer, eating sadza in Mbare or behind my uncle's butchery; the list is endless."

"You will forget all that once you are settled. There will be other forms of entertainment there. Maybe even more entertaining than what you are used to here," predicted Munya.

After drinking a few beers with his friends, Zvina excused himself and left. He wanted to get home early. He wanted to start planning his departure right away. Although he was excited about his visit to Canada, the fact that he had quit his job had suddenly caused him to be very anxious. On his way home, he started wondering what would happen if he found that he did not like Canada. If he came back home, he would not have a job. Would it be easy for him to find another job, given the state of the economy? He had learned that the immigration process takes up to eighteen months or even longer. What would he do if his application took that long? Where would he be? His visitor's visa would obviously expire well before the permanent residency application was finalized. That means he would have to leave Canada, since overstaying would jeopardize his permanent residency application. So, would he need to come back to Zimbabwe? Maybe quitting his job was not a good idea after all, he thought. He shook his head and said loudly,

"I made the right decision. If I had not quit my job, I would have an excuse to give up when the going gets tough. Now, I have no incentive to come back here. I will do everything I can to make sure I do not come back here. If I have to come back, it will be temporary. I will be waiting for my papers to get processed. There is no turning back. This is it. The worst thing that's going to happen is that I will end up going to South Africa. I will not stay here."

The next day Zvina went downtown to the travel agency he had chosen to book his flights with. When he arrived at the agency's reception area, a lady behind the reception desk greeted him.

"Good afternoon, Sir. How are you today?"

"I am fine, and you?" replied Zvina.

"I am fine, Sir. How may I help you today?" asked the lady.

"I would like to book some flights to Canada," replied Zvina.

"We can certainly help you with that. Take a seat, please," said the lady, pointing to some chairs that were next to the main entrance. "I will ask one of our international travel agents to help you."

"Thank you," replied Zvina, as he walked towards the chairs to take a seat.

The lady picked up the phone and had a brief conversation before assuring Zvina that one of their agents would be coming to help him in a few minutes. Zvina thanked her again and then got lost in his thoughts about the different flight options he would likely be presented with. The best flight for him would be a direct flight to Canada. He did not want any stops, especially in countries where visas or transit visas are required. He did not have the time to apply for visas. He did not need a visa for Canada, so he did not want to waste money and time applying for visas to countries that he was just passing through. He also did not like stops where he would have to spend some time in a hotel before catching his connecting flight. Even though most airlines paid for accommodation and food in such cases, he knew that he would somehow end up spending some of his money before arriving in Canada. On the other hand, such flights could be a lot cheaper than the more direct flights. That could save him some money. He realized that he would have to carefully consider all of the available options before making a decision. While Zvina was still lost in his thoughts, a female agent walked in.

"Hello, Sir. Please follow me to my office. I will help you." Zvina almost jumped out of the chair as he had not seen the agent walk in.

"Oh my God. You scared me. I did not see you coming in," said Zvina, as he stood up.

"Oh! I am so sorry, Sir. I did not mean to scare you. I did not realize that you had not seen me coming in," the agent apologized.

"No problem. I was daydreaming. That's why," said Zvina.

"Anyway, follow me to my office," said the agent.

They went into the agent's office. In the office, the agent offered Zvina a seat before she went to sit on the other side of the desk facing Zvina.

"Ok, Sir. Let me start by introducing myself. My name is Sarah. I am one of the two senior international travel agents at this branch. I have been with the company for over eight years now. I have been in the travel industry for over twelve years. I am glad to help make your travel arrangements to any destination in the world. How may I help you today?"

"Well, I would like to travel to Canada and come back after two months," replied Zvina.

"When do you want to depart, Sir?" asked the agent.

"In five weeks," Zvina replied.

"Which part of Canada are you going to?" the agent asked again.

"I am going to the city of Calgary in Alberta."

"I can get you flights to Calgary either through Europe or USA. The flights through Europe usually have fewer connecting flights, so your total travelling time would be less. For example, if you go through London or Amsterdam, I can get you flights with just the one stop in those cities. Would you prefer the flights through Europe?" asked the agent.

"Madam, I want the cheapest flights I can get, as long as I do not have to spend several days travelling. And I do not want to connect in countries where transit visas will be required, because I do not have the time to apply for the transit visas. I don't mind if it takes a day or so longer to get to my destination, as long as I avoid that," said Zvina, leaning over the agent's desk.

"Ok, Sir. I fully understand what you want. Leave it with me. I will find you the best three options, and then you can select from those. How does that sound?" asked the agent.

"Sounds good to me," replied Zvina.

"I would like an hour or so to work on this. Could you come back in two hours? If you can't, I can call you and give you the options over the phone. You can think about them and decide over the next few days. When you have made up your mind, you may come back, and then we will make the bookings," suggested the agent.

"No problem. Just call me when you have the options. I will come back with payment once I have decided on which option to choose," said Zvina as he stood up.

"Ok. Thank you, Sir. I will call you in two hours at the latest. See you then," said the agent. She reached out to give Zvina a handshake.

Later that afternoon, the agent called Zvina and presented him with the three options she had selected for him. The first option was to fly through London. This option would take the least amount of time but it was the priciest. The second option was to fly through Ghana with connecting flights in Accra, New York, and Toronto. This option would take the longest time, but it was the cheapest. The third option was to fly through South Africa with connecting flights in Johannesburg, Atlanta, and Seattle. This option would take less time than the second option but it was pricier. Zvina chose the second option.

After Zvina had bought his ticket, he knew there was no turning back. He was going to Canada. He had to do a couple of things before he left. He had to go to Gweru to get his money from the bullbar sales, as well as negotiate to have the car dealer buy any remaining bullbars at a discount price. He also had to sell his truck and pay back what he owed to his employer. He decided that he would go to Gweru first before he sold his truck. He did not want to travel to Gweru on public transport.

The next day he advertised his truck in the popular national newspaper. Then he left for Gweru. When he arrived at the dealership in Gweru, he was very pleased to find that there were only a few bullbars left.

"Hello, Mr. Mawira," George greeted Zvina as he entered his office.

George was the owner of the car dealership. He was a very nice guy who shared a good business relationship with Zvina.

"Hello, George. How are you?" replied Zvina, taking a seat in front of George's desk.

"I am very well, thank you. Why didn't you bring bullbars? I only have a few left, and I think they will be gone in less than two weeks."

"Yes, I saw that, but I have to talk to you about something."

"What is it, Zvina? Don't tell me you are quitting selling bullbars."

"Well, you are right," said Zvina, looking down. "I have decided to leave the country."

Zvina went on to tell George about his plans to leave the country. George gave him money for the bullbars that had been sold. After thanking George, Zvina offered to sell George the remaining bullbars at a thirty-five percent discount.

"No, Zvina. That's too much of a discount. You will make a loss on these bullbars."

"No problem. We have worked very well together, and we had such a good business relationship built on trust and fairness. This is my way of saying thank you. I will be gone by the time you sell these bullbars."

"But I can always send the money to your wife."

"Of course, but this is my way of thanking you for being such a good business partner. Please take the offer, even if you don't have the cash right now. You can send the payment to my wife when you sell the bars."

"Ok, Zvina. If you insist, I will take the offer. Thank you very much."

Zvina and George agreed on the deal, and then they went out for lunch together. Soon after lunch, Zvina left Gweru for Harare.

Over the next few days, Zvina got a few calls from potential buyers who wanted to see his truck. Soon he had a buyer and the truck was gone. He was happy to get a good deal from the sale. In fact, he sold the truck for more than he had paid for it because the rate of inflation in Zimbabwe was very high at that time. Prices were rising daily.

On the day that Zvina was supposed to leave for Canada, he invited his friends and relatives to his place for lunch. After lunch, they spent the rest of the afternoon at Zvina's place. Just before sunset, they all left for the airport to see Zvina off.

On the way to the airport, Zvina did not talk much. He was starting to get anxious. This was his first time going overseas. It would take him three days to get to Calgary. He wondered what he would occupy himself with during the three days of travel. He had packed a few books, but he was not a keen reader, and so he knew he would not be reading much. He had a sixteen-hour stopover in Ghana. He thought that would give him an opportunity to see Accra. He had read about Accra in high school. He pictured a very old densely populated city. He thought about the famous New York City. Unfortunately, he would not see much of it since he would not be leaving the airport. He did not have a U.S. visa.

When they arrived at the airport, there was a long queue at the Ghana Airways check-in counter. Zvina joined the queue with his wife and son. After checking in, Zvina and his wife and son joined their relatives in the Departures Hall. Zvina bade everybody farewell and left for the Departures Lounge.

Chapter Four

Stranded in Ghana

After eating dinner in the little restaurant at the hotel, Zvina went back to his room and packed up his belongings. He went to the reception desk, checked out, and waited for the airport shuttle in the lobby. At exactly eight p.m. the shuttle arrived. Zvina boarded the shuttle along with other guests who were also going back to Kotoka International airport. At the airport, Zvina proceeded to the USA-bound Ghana Airways check-in queue. It was a very long queue, so it took Zvina about thirty minutes to get to the check-in counter.

"Hello, Sir. May I have your ticket and passport please?" asked the agent.

Zvina reached out to give the agent his ticket and passport.

"What is your final destination, Sir?"

"Canada," replied Zvina.

"Where in Canada?" asked the agent again.

"Calgary, Alberta," replied Zvina.

"And you are passing through the USA?"

"Yes."

"I don't see any American or Canadian visas in your passport," said the agent with a frown.

"Zimbabweans don't need to get a visa before travelling to Canada. I will get the visa at the port of entry. In the USA, I will not be leaving the airport. I do not have to pass through immigration," replied Zvina, smiling.

"What is the purpose of your visit to Canada?" the agent asked again.

"I am visiting my uncle."

"Does your uncle work?"

"Yes, he does. He owns a fashion store."

"How much money are you taking with you to Canada?"

"I have one thousand U.S. dollars."

"That's not enough money to fund your stay in Canada for two months."

"I know. But this is just pocket money. Like I said, I am visiting my uncle. I will not be paying for accommodation and I will not be buying food. My uncle is hosting me."

"Sir! How can I confirm that you are telling the truth? You need to show me that you have sufficient funds to pay for your stay in Canada."

"But I told you I will not be paying for accommodation and food. My uncle will be providing that."

"Sir! I don't want to argue with you. Please step aside. I have to serve other travellers. I will come back to you after we have cleared the queue. You may go and sit over there," said the agent, pointing to a nearby bench.

After all of the other travellers had checked in, the agent left the counter and went into an office that was located next to the security check entrance. At that time Zvina started to get anxious about what was happening. He remained seated and told himself to be patient. After a while, the agent came out and signalled for Zvina to come back to the check-in desk.

"Sir, like I said before, I need proof that you have sufficient funds to pay for your stay in Canada," said the agent in a very assertive tone.

Zvina looked at her in disbelief, and shook his head.

"Madam, I have told you already. Ok. Here is an invitation letter my uncle sent me which states that he will be responsible for my food and board while I am in Canada," said Zvina, as he reached into his little bag to pull out his documents.

"That will not help, Sir," said the agent. She continued, "How do I know it's your uncle who wrote that email?"

"Ok, Madam. Shall I give you his phone number so you can call him?" asked Zvina, showing signs of frustration.

"Sir, it's expensive to phone Canada. I am not allowed to make such calls. It's your responsibility to prove to me that you have enough funds to cover your expenses in Canada," replied the agent.

"There is no other way I can think of," said Zvina.

"In that case, Sir, I cannot let you fly on Ghana Airways to USA," said the agent.

"What?" asked Zvina in disbelief. "When I bought my ticket my travel agent told me that since I had my uncle's invitation letter I would not have any problems. I don't understand why this should be a problem here. I shouldn't have been allowed to board the Ghana Airways flight from Harare in the first place. Can I talk your supervisor, please?"

"That won't help you, Sir. He will tell you exactly what I have told you," answered the agent.

"No. This does not make sense. I demand to see your supervisor," said Zvina. His shaky voice clearly conveyed his frustration and impatience.

"Ok, Sir. I will call my supervisor," said the agent, leaving the check-in desk.

The agent went into a nearby office and closed the door behind her. Zvina stood by the counter waiting for the agent to come back with her supervisor. As time went by with no one showing up, Zvina became increasingly impatient and agitated. He started pacing back and forth in front of the check-in desk. After some time, a man came out of the office to the check-in desk.

"Hello, Sir," the man greeted Zvina. "I am told you want to see me. I am the check-in desk supervisor. How may I help you?"

"I am supposed to fly on Ghana Airways to New York tonight enroute to Toronto, Canada. The agent who served me here says she cannot check me in because I have no proof of sufficient funds to pay for my food and board in Canada, and because I do not have a transit visa for USA. When I bought my ticket back in Zimbabwe, my agent told me that I did not need a transit visa for USA because I will not be leaving the airport. As for proof of funds, I told your agent that I will be staying with my uncle, who will be providing me with food and accommodation. The money I have on me is just pocket money. When I checked in at Harare International Airport, the agent asked me the same questions and I gave her the same answers. She checked me in without any issues. I am surprised that there are issues now. By the way, I flew Ghana Airways from Zimbabwe and they put me into a hotel when I arrived here because my next flight, this flight, was almost twenty hours away. If Ghana Airways allowed me to fly from Zimbabwe, then why am I not allowed to continue with my journey? What has changed? Could you please explain to me what's going on here?" Zvina was literally shaking with anger and frustration as he explained his case to the check-in desk supervisor.

"Thank you for explaining this to me, Sir. May I have your travel documents please?" asked the check-in desk supervisor.

Zvina pulled out his travel documents from his small bag and handed them over to the supervisor.

"I will be right back, Sir. I just need to go and talk to the agent who served you so I can understand why she is not checking you in," said the supervisor.

"But my flight is boarding now. I have a bag that has to be checked in. It will not make it through baggage handling in time to catch the flight," said Zvina, sounding very desperate.

"Sir! I must follow procedures and protocols. There is nothing I can do. You just have to wait until I get back." The supervisor turned around and went back into the office.

Zvina looked at his watch. It was just ten minutes before departure time, which meant the gate was closing. He realized that he was not going to get onto this flight. He paced back and forth in front of the check-in counter for a few minutes before sitting on his large travelling bag. At that point, he started asking himself a lot of questions.

"Did I do anything wrong here? No, I don't think I did anything wrong. My travel documents are in order. If they were not, they wouldn't have allowed me to fly from Harare in the first place. So, what is it? Were all my relatives happy to see me leaving Zimbabwe? Maybe someone was not happy and they used juju to cast some bad luck on me. But why me? I am not the first person in the family to go overseas. Maybe it's just bad luck. Oh! By the way, I am in West Africa. I once heard that in West Africa, if you do not want to have any problems with customs and immigration officials, you have to put some American money in your passport before you hand it over to the agents. They get the money and stamp your passport and let you go without any questions. That might be the reason. I did not put any money in my passport. Maybe I should have. Anyway, let's hear what he has to say."

While Zvina was still asking himself these questions, the supervisor came back holding Zvina's documents in his hands.

"Sir, I have had a look at your documents and what the agent said still stands. You need a transit visa for USA, and you need proof that you have sufficient funds to pay for your stay in Canada," said the supervisor as he approached Zvina.

"This is ridiculous," said Zvina, once again revealing his anger and frustration. "Officer, I need to know why I was allowed to board Ghana Airways in Harare in the first place. I was asked these questions and I gave the same answers. I was told that all was ok and they allowed me to board the plane. Somebody has to explain this to me and take responsibility for this," stammered Zvina, trying to hold back his tears.

"Sir, I cannot help you. The only advice I can give you is to go to the American Embassy tomorrow and get a transit visa and get someone, maybe your uncle in Canada, to send you a bank statement which shows that he has enough funds to pay for your stay in Canada," said the supervisor.

"This is not acceptable. I demand to see your superiors," demanded Zvina.

"I am the most senior person on duty. Whatever I say goes. The flight you were supposed to catch is departing right now. So, be rest assured that you are not flying out of Accra tonight," said the supervisor. "I will call for a shuttle from the hotel where you stayed to come and pick you up. First thing tomorrow morning, go and get the transit visa at the USA Embassy. After that, ask your uncle to fax you his bank statement. We have another flight departing for New York at the same time tomorrow. We will try and get you onto that one," said the supervisor, trying to console Zvina.

He passed the documents back to Zvina and went back into his office. After a few minutes, he came out and advised Zvina that he had called for a shuttle to pick him up and take him back to the hotel.

"I did not have to pay for my stay at the hotel last time. Who is going to pay for my stay tonight?" asked Zvina.

"You are on your own, Sir. Ghana Airways is not responsible for what happened to you. It's your responsibility to ensure that you have the required documents when you travel."

"For sure," replied Zvina. "But in this case, it was Ghana Airways' responsibility to ensure that I did not board their plane in Harare since I did not have the required documents. I think Ghana Airways should accept responsibility for what's happening to me. They should pay for my accommodation and food."

"It's Ghana Airways' policy. I will not argue with you, Sir. Just do as I advised and come back at the same time tomorrow evening. The shuttle has arrived. See you tomorrow evening, and good luck with the visa application," said the supervisor sarcastically as he walked back to his office.

Zvina watched the supervisor walk away before picking up

his baggage and heading towards one of the exits. The same shuttle that had brought him and the other travellers to the airport was parked outside. As Zvina approached the shuttle, the shuttle driver jumped out to help him with his baggage.

"Oh sir! It's you?" exclaimed the shuttle driver in surprise. "What happened? There is no way you could have missed your flight. We were here on time," said the shuttle driver.

"There were some issues regarding my travel documents. So, they wouldn't let me fly," replied Zvina.

"Ok. I am sorry to hear that. Are you going to be able to fix those issues here in Accra?"

"Yes, I think I can. I just need a transit visa for the USA. I also have to ask my uncle in Canada to fax me his bank statement which shows that he has enough money to look after me while I am there."

"That's good. If you have questions or need any help, just let me know. In fact, I can get someone with a cab to drive you to the USA Embassy in the morning. What time do you want to go?"

"I will have to think about it. What time does the Embassy open?" asked Zvina.

"I am not sure, but it must be nine o'clock," guessed the shuttle driver. He pulled out of the parking lot and drove back to the hotel.

When they arrived at the hotel, Zvina checked in and went straight to bed. He was sure it would be a struggle to fall asleep. His mind was in a state of confusion because of what had just happened. He was also considering what he should do next. As advised by the agent at the airport, he should go and apply for a transit visa at the USA Embassy. However, he was not sure if this was the right thing to do.

The Long Trip To Canada

He wondered if maybe he should go to the Ghana Airways offices and present his case. This plan made more sense to Zvina, because Ghana Airways had allowed him to board the flight from Harare without any issue. There was no reason why there should be an issue with his travel documents now. If there was, then Ghana Airways should take responsibility for getting him in this situation in the first place. He also thought about calling his agent back in Zimbabwe and asking her for advice. That sounded like a good idea. After all, she was the one who had told him that he didn't need a transit visa for the USA in the first place. He also wondered if his wife could send him money from Zimbabwe.

After spending a couple of hours pondering over the best way forward, Zvina finally fell asleep.

In the morning, Zvina woke up to the beautiful sound of singing birds. He slowly lifted his head off the pillow to check the time on the clock by his bedside. He was shocked to see that it was already after eight a.m. He jumped out of bed, brushed his teeth, and showered. Within a few minutes he was on his way to the hotel restaurant where he ate a quick breakfast. Back in his room, he sat down on the bed and thought about what he had to do that day in order to be allowed to proceed on his journey to Canada. There were a number of options that he could choose from. However, he had to seriously think about his chances of success with each one of them before making a decision. So, he took out his notebook from his bag and started writing things down.

The first option was to go to the USA Embassy and apply for the transit visa. This is what the agent at the airport had advised him, so maybe this would be easy. The application fee for the visa would not be very much, probably less than fifty U.S. dollars. He could afford that. But the problem is that visa applications do not usually get processed on the same day. Where would he stay while the visa was being processed? If he stayed in a hotel, he would quickly run out of money. That would worsen his other problem, given that the agents were insisting that he provide sufficient proof that he could pay for his stay in Canada. After thinking it over, Zvina reasoned that since the agents at the airport had advised him to go to the USA Embassy, they knew that he could get the visa on the same day.

The second option was to go to the Ghana Airways office, ask to speak to a senior employee, and present his case. He would argue that for the same reason he was allowed to fly from Harare, he should be allowed to proceed with his journey. If Ghana Airways would not allow him to proceed with his journey, then they were responsible for flying him back to Zimbabwe and refunding his ticket. They would also have to pay for his food and stay at the hotel for the time that he was in Ghana.

The third option was to call his travel agent in Harare and explain his situation to her. He would ask her why she had told him that he did not need a transit visa for USA, considering that the Ghana Airways officials were not allowing him to proceed with his journey for that reason. He would ask her to give him advice on how to solve this problem. She was a very knowledgeable travel consultant, and so she should be able to help him.

Zvina sat on the bed and pondered for thirty minutes before deciding which option to choose. In the end, he decided to go the USA Embassy and apply for the transit visa. He went to the hotel's reception desk and asked to have a cab called for him. The cab showed up within a few minutes. The driver came into the lobby and asked who had called for a cab.

"It was me," replied Zvina. "Can you please take me to the American Embassy?"

"My pleasure, Sir," replied the cab driver. "Come on. Let's go."

When they arrived at the American Embassy, the driver parked outside the gate and told Zvina how much he had to pay for the taxi ride.

"Ok, but can you please wait here for a few minutes? I need to find out how long it will take to get what I want here. If we find out how long it will take, then you could come back and pick me up when I am finished," suggested Zvina as he got out of the cab.

"No problem, Sir. I will wait," replied the cab driver.

The gate was closed but a security officer was seated in a little cabin by the gate. As Zvina walked towards the gate, he was suddenly gripped with fear. The atmosphere surrounding him felt heavy. He started sweating. He wondered if the officer would let him in. Generally, security officers are notorious for refusing people entry. It's very difficult to pass by them, especially if you do not have a host inside who can tell them to let you in. Zvina concluded that this would be a challenge. Nevertheless, he proceeded to the little cabin.

"Good morning, Officer," he greeted the security officer.

"Good morning," the officer replied. "How can I help you?"

"I would like to go inside the Embassy. Can you please let me in?"

"What do you want to do in the Embassy? Do you have an appointment?" asked the officer.

"No, I don't have an appointment. I would like to apply for a transit visa. I am travelling to Canada but I am passing through New York. So, I need a transit visa," explained Zvina.

"Do you have all the required documents and the application fees?"

"Yes, I do," replied Zvina getting his travel documents out of his bag.

"Let's see them," said the officer.

Zvina handed the officer his travel documents. The officer only looked at Zvina's passport before handing the documents back.

"You are not Ghanaian!" exclaimed the officer.

"No, I am not Ghanaian. I am Zimbabwean," replied Zvina.

"We can't help you here," said the officer.

"Why?" asked Zvina in disbelief.

"This office does not process visas for non-Ghanaians. You have to go back and apply for the visa at the American Embassy in your country," replied the officer.

"Officer, I can't go back to Zimbabwe. I left Zimbabwe the day before yesterday on my way to Canada. When I left Zimbabwe, I was told that all was well and that I did not need a transit visa for USA since I would not be leaving the airport in New York. But when I arrived here, things had apparently changed. Ghana Airways won't let me fly if I don't have the U.S. transit visa. Can I please talk to someone in the Embassy just to confirm if I do really need the transit visa?" Zvina politely asked the officer.

"My friend, I cannot let you in just for that reason. If Ghana Airways tells you that you need a visa, then you need one. Unfortunately, like I said, you can't get that visa here," replied the officer.

"I just thought that if I explained my situation to somebody at the Embassy, they would be able to help. I can't go back to Zimbabwe," insisted Zvina.

"My friend, if I were you I would be on my way back to Zimbabwe. Don't waste your time here, because I am not going to let you in," asserted the officer.

Zvina sighed heavily, turned around, and walked towards the cab. He was devastated.

"So how long are you going to take, Sir?" asked the cab driver.

"Never mind," replied Zvina, opening the passenger door. "Just take me back to the hotel, please."

"What did they say?" asked the cab driver. "They can't give you the visa?"

"No, they can't," replied Zvina. "They said that I have to go back to my country."

"Oh! You are not Ghanaian?"

"No. I am not. I am Zimbabwean," replied Zvina.

When they arrived at the hotel, Zvina paid for the cab ride and went straight to his room. He had some thinking to do and he was running out of time. If he missed the flight that night, which was a Tuesday, the next flight was three days away. This would make his situation even worse as he would spend a good portion of his travel budget on food and hotel bills during those next three days. He had to come up with a solution before it was too late. He decided that he needed to go to the Ghana Airways office at the airport and talk to some senior officials. He did not want to waste time, so he left his room and went to the lobby. At the reception desk, he met the shuttle driver who had driven him to and from the airport the previous night.

"Good morning, Sir," the shuttle driver greeted Zvina.

"Good morning," replied Zvina.

"Did you go to the USA Embassy?" asked the shuttle driver.

"Yes, I did," replied Zvina.

"Did you get the visa?"

"No, I didn't."

"What are you going to do? You can't go back to Zimbabwe. You have to proceed with your journey to Canada," said the shuttle driver.

"Well, I guess the next thing I can try is to go to the Ghana Airways office at the airport and present my case to a senior official. They should be able to help me. If they let me fly from Zimbabwe, there is no reason why they should stop me from proceeding with my journey from here. If they made a mistake by letting me fly from Zimbabwe, then they are responsible for what's happening to me. They should provide the solution to my problem," reasoned Zvina.

"I understand what you are saying, but you will get the same answer from any senior official you talk to at Ghana Airways. I know those people," said the shuttle driver.

"If they cannot allow me to proceed with my journey, then they should pay for my food and accommodation here until they fly me back to Zimbabwe. They have to pay for the flight as well. I need to talk to them ASAP so that if I have to go back to Zimbabwe, I can leave on the next available flight. The sooner I return to Zimbabwe, the sooner I can apply for the transit visa and proceed with my journey. Ghana Airways must refund my ticket or move it to a future date, so I can

The Long Trip To Canada

use it once I get the visa. I think I should talk to them rather than try any other alternatives," said Zvina.

"I think what you need, Sir, is to call your travel agent back in Zimbabwe and tell her what's happening. When she booked the ticket, she was obviously told what documentation was required for her customer to fly from Zimbabwe to Canada without issues. If you meet the requirements that she was told at the time of purchasing the ticket, then there is no issue. Ghana Airways has to let you proceed with your trip. She is in a better position to argue that point than you. She knows the industry well and she knows the right person to talk to at Ghana Airways. I think you have a better chance for a positive outcome if you do it that way," advised the shuttle driver.

"Ok. I will take your advice. I will do that," said Zvina, standing up. He added, "I guess I will come back and see you after I have talked to my travel agent. I may ask you to take me to the airport."

"I am sorry, but I can't. I only take people who are flying. You have to get a taxi," replied the shuttle driver.

"Ok. Thanks."

Zvina went back to his room and called his agent in Zimbabwe.

"Hello. May I speak to Sarah, please?" asked Zvina as he sat down on the bed.

"Sarah has gone for lunch. Would you like to leave a message, Sir?" replied the lady on the other end of the line.

"What time does she get back from lunch?" asked Zvina. He sighed, lying down on the bed.

"She should be back in the next thirty minutes."

"Ok. I will call back in thirty minutes. Thank you," said Zvina, putting the phone down.

The thirty-minute wait felt like a very long time for Zvina. He felt that this was his lifeline that would determine whether or not he could proceed with his journey to Canada. Sarah had told him that he did not need a transit visa for the U.S., and that she had confirmed this fact with both the U.S. Embassy in Zimbabwe and Ghana Airways. She would know the right people to talk to.

After thirty minutes Zvina picked up the phone and called again.

"Hello. May I speak with Sarah please?" he asked.

"Yes. Please hold for Sarah," replied the lady who had answered the phone before.

Zvina jumped off the bed, covered the phone's mouthpiece, and screamed, "Yes!"

"Hello. This is Sarah speaking. How may I help you today?"

"Hello, Sarah. This is Zvina. You made my travel arrangements to Canada this month and I left Zimbabwe last Sunday."

"Oh yes, I remember. How are you? Are you in Canada?" asked Sarah.

"No, Sarah. I am stuck in Accra."

"Why? What happened?" Sarah asked again.

Zvina went on to explain to Sarah what had happened to him when he wanted to board the flight to New York the previous night. He also told her about his trip to the U.S. Embassy.

"Ok, Zvina. Calm down. I will fix this. Give me the phone number of the hotel where you are right now. I will call you back once I have talked to the Ghana Airways officials," said Sarah.

Zvina gave Sarah the phone number as well as his room number. Sarah reassured him that she would do her best to resolve this issue as soon as possible. She would also file a complaint to have Ghana Airways pay for all the costs Zvina had incurred since he had missed his flight as well as the costs he would be incurring until they got him on a flight to proceed with his journey.

"Ok, Zvina. I will get back to you ASAP. Like I said, calm down and don't worry. I will get this resolved. You are not coming back to Zimbabwe. You are proceeding with your trip to Canada. Bye for now," Sarah reassured Zvina again before hanging up.

Up to this point, Zvina had not wanted to tell his wife and his relatives what was happening. He thought they would be worried about him, especially his wife. However, after speaking with Sarah, he was confident that there was a solution in sight. He called his wife and told her what was going on. Jill was very disappointed, but he reassured her that he would be fine. Sarah would straighten things out for him, so that he could continue with his journey.

Zvina put the phone down and threw himself back on the bed. As he lay on the bed, his mind was stormed by a whirlwind of possibilities. Sarah had assured him that she would get the Ghana Airways authorities to allow him to proceed with his journey. Would this be the end of his problems on this journey? Or was this just the beginning? What would happen when he landed in New York? Would he not have similar problems with the American authorities? If he managed to proceed to Toronto, what would happen when he got there? His ticket would bring him to Toronto, not Calgary. The plan was to buy the ticket from Toronto to Calgary in Toronto. Sarah had offered this suggestion as a cost-savings measure. But would this inevitably create problems in Toronto? While he was thinking about all these worries, he fell into a deep sleep and started dreaming.

In his dream, Zvina called the shuttle driver and asked to be driven to the airport. At the airport, he went straight to the check-in counter and checked in without any issues. He proceeded to the security checkpoint and passed through without any issues. When he entered the Departures Lounge, his plane was already boarding, so he proceeded to the boarding gate and went on board. He was surprised to find that his seat was in business class. As he stood next to his seat, he was greeted by a flight attendant who offered him a drink.

"Scotch on the rocks, please," he told the attendant.

The flight attendant left and then returned with a glass of whisky. He handed the glass to Zvina, who accepted it with a wide grin on his face. He took a sip and placed the glass on the table. He looked around, picked up the TV controller, and turned on the little TV in front of him. He also noticed a phone handset next to the TV controller. As he flipped through channels on the TV and took occasional sips of the whisky, the phone handset started ringing. He tried to pick up the handset to answer the call, but a big strong man grabbed his hand and told him not to answer it. Zvina wrestled the man and jumped out of his seat.

At that moment he woke up and jumped off the bed. His room phone was ringing. Still breathing heavily from the brief ordeal in his dream, he answered the phone.

"Hello. Zvina speaking. Can I help you?"

"Hi, Zvina. It's Sarah here."

The Long Trip To Canada

"Oh Sarah! I was fast asleep. I fell asleep after talking to you. So, tell me. What did you find out for me?"

"Ok. I called Ghana Airways office here in Harare and explained what happened to you. They were actually surprised that you were not allowed to proceed with your journey. They called their office in Ghana to make arrangements to have you on the next available flight to New York. There is a flight to New York tonight, but unfortunately, it's full. The next available flight is in three days. They will book you onto that one. Your connecting flight to Toronto has also been confirmed. You are good to go."

"No. No. No, Sarah! Who is going to pay for my hotel bill and food for the next three days? I can't afford to use my money. I may need to prove that I have the money to buy my ticket from Toronto to Calgary when I get to Canada," said Zvina.

"You are getting ahead of me, Zvina. I am getting to that. Ghana Airways has accepted responsibility for what happened to you. They will pay all your hotel, food, and transportation expenses from the day you missed the flight until they get you on the flight to New York. I want you to go to Ghana Airways office at the airport and see a manager called Mrs. Aning. She is expecting you. She has been given all of your details including your ticket number and your final destination. She will explain to you what's happening from today until they fly you out of there," explained Sarah.

"Ok, Sarah. How about in New York? Will I have problems in New York because I do not have a transit visa?" asked Zvina, seeking reassurance.

"No. You will not have any problems. You are not leaving the airport, so you won't have to pass through immigration. You won't officially enter USA," replied Sarah.

"Ok, Sarah. Thank you very much. I will go to the airport right now. I think I will have peace of mind once I talk to this lady."

"Everything is fine now, Zvina. Trust me. Anyway, if you encounter any more problems, please give me a call ASAP. I don't want you to miss the next flight. I will have probably left my office by the time you get back from the airport this afternoon, but I will give you a call as soon as I get back to the office tomorrow morning. Talk to you then. Bye for now."

Zvina put down the phone, picked up his little bag containing his travel documents, and left the room. At the reception desk, the receptionist called a taxi for him and within a few moments he was on his way to the airport. The taxi dropped him off at Ghana Airways' office.

"Good afternoon. My name is Zvina Mawira. I am here to see Mrs. Aning."

"Good afternoon," replied the lady at the front desk. "Is she expecting you, Sir?" the lady went on to ask.

"Yes. I have been told she is expecting me," replied Zvina.

"Ok. Take a seat, Sir. I will let her know that you are here."

The lady disappeared into the hallway behind the reception desk. Although he had been asked to take a seat, Zvina did not sit down. He was growing increasingly anxious. He could not wait to see Mrs. Aning. He kept pacing back and forth in front of the front desk. Within a few minutes, the lady emerged from the hallway.

"Sir, I said you can take a seat. She is busy right now, but she will be free in a few minutes. She will come and get you," said the lady.

"Ok. Thank you," replied Zvina, finally taking a seat.

After about ten minutes, Mrs. Aning came to the reception area.

"Are you Mr. Mawira?" she asked, as she approached Zvina.

"Yes, I am," replied Zvina, as he stood up.

"Well hello," she said, reaching out to shake hands with Zvina, "My name is Mrs. Aning. Please come to my office with me."

As they walked to Mrs. Aning's office, Zvina's heart started beating faster again. This is the moment he had been waiting for. However, his first impression of Mrs. Aning was of somebody who does not bring good news. She had a serious look and did not smile at all. He was desperate to hear what she had to say. The short walk to Mrs. Aning's office felt like a thousand miles.

"Take a seat, Sir," said Mrs. Aning, showing Zvina to a chair in front of her desk.

As Zvina sat down, he was literally shivering. He was scared that Mrs. Aning might not have good news for him.

"Well, Zvina. I have been told about your whole ordeal at the airport last night," said Mrs. Aning, pulling out her chair to sit down.

Zvina looked at her and nodded a few times.

"I must begin by apologizing to you on behalf of Ghana Airways," Mrs. Aning continued, to Zvina's surprise. He could not believe that statement.

"We are very sorry that you were not allowed to board last night's flight to New York as per your travel arrangements. We allowed you to board the flight from Zimbabwe based on the information you provided us which we deemed to be adequate to allow you to pass through USA and enter Canada without any issues. We are obligated to see to it that you get to your final destination. However, I would like to kindly ask you to show me all your travel documents, so I can confirm before we move on to talk about what's going to happen next."

Zvina pulled out his travel documents from his bag and handed them over to Mrs. Aning. He did not say a word. He was still in shock and disbelief. Mrs. Aning took the documents and perused through them one at a time. When she was done, she handed them back to Zvina before asking, "How much cash do you have on you, Mr. Mawira?"

Zvina replied, "Just under one thousand dollars U.S. I had one thousand, but I had to use some of it for taxi fares and food."

"Ok. That should be fine. Now, Mr. Mawira, the next flight to New York from Accra is in three days at midnight. We have booked you on that flight. This means you will be in Accra for the next three days. You will arrive in New York in the afternoon and have a four-hour stopover before you catch your connecting flight to Toronto. You will arrive in Toronto late evening on the same day. Like I said before, we recognize the inconvenience we have caused you. Ghana Airways will pay for your food and accommodation expenses in Accra until we fly you out. You will stay at the same hotel and we kindly ask that you have your meals at this hotel. We want to keep the process simple. We do not want you to use your own money and then have to claim it. If you use your own money on food, it will not be reimbursed. For your travel between the airport and the hotel, please use the hotel shuttle. Do you have any questions?"

"Yes, Madam. When I come to the airport on the day of my departure, do I just proceed to check-in like the other passengers?" asked Zvina.

"Yes. I will ensure that all staff at the check-in desk are aware that you will be coming and to expect you. You won't have any problems," replied Mrs. Aning.

"Ok, thanks," said Zvina.

"Good! You can go back to the hotel and relax for the next three days. On your departure day, please come to the airport early. I would prefer that you are among the first to check-in and pass through security. Then you may relax in the Departures Lounge. You will have a long journey ahead of you," advised Mrs. Aning.

"Ok. Thanks for your advice. I will do that," replied Zvina.

"Ok. Great! I will walk you to the reception area."

Zvina stood up and exited the office ahead of Mrs. Aning. He was so relieved, he felt like jumping up and screaming with joy.

"It's unfortunate that you can't spend any of your money while you are here. You could have visited a few places of interest in Accra. It will be boring for you to sit and hang around that little hotel for three days. I really feel sorry for you," said Mrs. Aning.

"I know, but there is nothing I can do. I guess I will have to watch TV and go for long walks when I am tired of watching TV," replied Zvina.

"Ok, Zvina. It was nice meeting you. I wish you safe travels. The receptionist here will call the hotel shuttle for you," said Mrs. Aning, giving Zvina a handshake.

"Thank you very much for your help on this issue. I look forward to my next flight. It was nice meeting you too, and once again, thank you," said Zvina.

"Just give me a minute, Sir. I will call to find out where the shuttle is," said the receptionist as she picked up the phone.

After a brief moment on the phone, she hung up and told Zvina that the shuttle was at the Arrivals parking lot. Zvina thanked her and left for the Arrivals parking lot. When he arrived at the parking lot, he went to the shuttle and found no one inside. He sat down on the curb next to the shuttle and waited for the shuttle driver to come. After a short while, the shuttle driver finally came with four other passengers. He opened the shuttle door and helped the passengers load their luggage into the shuttle before turning to Zvina.

"Hello, Sir. I guess you want to go back to the hotel. Did you manage to get your issue resolved?" the shuttle driver asked.

"Yes, I did," replied Zvina.

"Thank God. That's good news. So, when are you proceeding with your journey?" he asked again.

"In three days," replied Zvina.

"That's not too bad. Anyway, get in, and I will take you all to the hotel," said the shuttle driver as he walked to the other side of the shuttle.

Zvina got into the shuttle and went to sit at the back. He did not want the shuttle driver to keep talking to him because he was likely going to keep talking about what had happened to him. He did not want the other passengers to know what had happened to him.

While seated quietly on the back seat, Zvina started thinking about what he would do for the next three days. He was very limited in his options because he did not want to spend his money. He planned to do exactly what he had told Mrs. Aning: watch TV and go for long walks. They arrived at the hotel just before sunset, and Zvina went to his room. He had a quick shower and went to the reception desk. He wanted to confirm that Ghana Airways had contacted them about his case and that they would be footing his food and accommodation bill at the hotel. After confirming this with the receptionist, he had dinner in the hotel restaurant before going back to his room.

After watching TV in his room for some time, he realized that it was going to be a long night. And given what had happened that day, he had every reason to celebrate. Spending a few dollars from his pocket money on a few beers was not going to make a difference. He went to the bar at the hotel and had a few beers with some other hotel guests before going back to his room to sleep.

The three days passed by faster than Zvina had anticipated. He spent most of his time watching TV in his room. On his last day at the hotel, he had an early dinner, checked out, and caught the shuttle to the airport well ahead of the check-in time. He wanted to be among the first passengers to check-in. Although he had been promised that he would not experience any more problems, he was still somewhat apprehensive that he might run into the same problem again.

When he arrived at the airport, there were two passengers ahead of him in the queue waiting to check-in. He joined the queue. After waiting for about half an hour, the check-in desk opened and they started checking in passengers. At the check-in desk, Zvina handed his travel documents to the agent and quietly waited for any questions.

"How are you today?" asked the agent.

"I am fine, and you?" replied Zvina.

"I am fine," replied the agent as she perused through Zvina's passport.

"Ahh. Mr. Mawira? We have been told to expect you. What's your final destination, by the way?" asked the agent.

"Canada," replied Zvina.

"Ok. All is good. Please place your baggage on the scale," said the agent, handing the documents back to Zvina.

Zvina placed his big travelling bag on the scale.

"Looks good. Here are your two boarding passes: one for New York, and the other for Toronto. You can proceed to security and then to the Departures Lounge. Enjoy your trip," said the agent, handing Zvina his boarding passes.

"Thank you very much," said Zvina as he accepted the boarding passes.

Zvina quickly proceeded to security and passed through without any issues. He was so relieved that he was finally leaving Accra and continuing with his trip. "This calls for a celebration," he thought. He went straight to the bar in the Departures Lounge to drink to this "milestone" in his quest to get to Canada. While sitting in the bar and drinking, he started thinking about his wife and son back home. It was going to be at least a couple of months before he returned to Zimbabwe. That was a long time. He had not been away from his wife and son for that long since the son was born. If things worked out the way he wanted, that time was probably going to be longer. If he ended up staying in Canada, it was obviously going to take more than two months before his wife and son could join him. He had to work out a plan to reunite with his family as soon as possible. However, he would not jeopardize his family's chances of emigrating to Canada. He would rather be away from them for some time, as long as the final goal of moving to Canada would eventually be realized. While he was still lost in his thoughts, he heard the boarding call for his flight. He quickly paid his bill and headed to the Departure gate.

Chapter Five

Welcome to North America

The noise from the clapping and ululating passengers woke Zvina up. He could not figure out why the other passengers were clapping and ululating, so he turned to the passenger next to him and asked, "Why are they clapping and ululating?"

"We have landed in New York. They are thanking the pilots for a safe flight," replied the other passenger.

"Oh. I see," said Zvina.

When they got off the plane, Zvina did not know what to do. He went to the information desk to ask for help.

"Hello. I just got off the flight from Ghana. I am supposed to connect to Toronto. Can you help me find my way to the right terminal, please?" Zvina asked the agent at the information desk.

"Can I have your ticket or boarding pass for the connecting flight, Sir?" asked the agent.

Zvina handed her the boarding pass.

"You need to go to Terminal Four. You must collect your baggage and get out of this terminal. Outside the terminal, you will see shuttles that transport travellers between terminals. Get onto one that will take you to Terminal Four," said the agent.

"Thank you," said Zvina, leaving the information desk. He proceeded to the baggage collection area and collected his baggage. He followed the exit signs, but to his surprise, he realized he was passing through customs. He wanted to stop and ask somebody for help, but there was no one to ask except for the other passengers. So, he decided to proceed. He would ask the customs officer how he could find his way to the terminal without "entering" USA, since he did not have a visa.

When he got to one of the customs desks, the officer asked for his passport. He handed him the passport and started explaining.

"Officer, I am not visiting USA. I am in transit to Canada. I don't have a U.S. visitor's visa. I just need to get to Terminal Four to catch my connecting flight."

"I see. But you have to get out of this terminal to go to Terminal Four, and for you to get out of this terminal, you have to "enter" USA. And so, you need a visa," explained the officer.

"Oh my God," said Zvina. He took a deep breath. "When I bought my ticket in Zimbabwe, I was told that I did not need a visa because I would not be officially entering USA. I would just be catching my connecting flight without passing through customs," he tried to explain.

"That's not going to happen, Sir. You have to pass through customs to get to your connecting flight's terminal," reiterated the officer.

"What should I do now, Officer?" asked Zvina, looking desperate and confused.

"May I have your boarding pass and ticket for the connecting flight, please?" asked the officer.

Zvina quickly handed him the documents and then went on to ask, "Is it possible to get a transit visa here?"

"No, Sir," replied the officer as he analyzed Zvina's documents. "You have to get the visa at the American Embassy in your home country."

"I wish I had known this. It was all my travel agent's fault. She insisted that I did not need a visa if I did not have to leave the airport. She said that I would just have to find my way to my connecting flight's Departures gate without passing through customs," Zvina tried to keep explaining.

"She was probably right in that you could do that at other airports, but certainly not here," said the officer.

"What can I do now?" Zvina asked the officer again.

"Please sit down on that bench over there. I will review your case with my supervisor and get back to you," said the officer, pointing to a bench behind Zvina.

The officer left his desk with Zvina's documents. Zvina, with a heavy heart and a sense of déjà vu, went over to the bench and sat down.

After about fifteen minutes the officer came back and asked Zvina to come over to his desk. There was a security officer standing next to him.

"I have reviewed your case with my supervisor," the officer said, staring at Zvina sternly. He continued, "Usually if a traveller does not have a visa and they want to enter America, we do not allow them to do so. In fact, we detain them and send them back to their home country on the next available flight.

However, your situation is a little different. We understand that at some airports you can connect flights without having to pass through customs. We will ask a security officer to escort you to your departure terminal. The officer will stay with you until you board your flight to Canada. I will not give you your documents. The security officer will keep them and hand them over to the flight captain. Your documents will be returned to you when the plane is airborne. Do you understand?"

"Yes, I do," replied Zvina.

Just a few metres away from them, Zvina noticed three armed security officers handcuffing a man and leading him away. For a moment, Zvina thought the same thing was going to happen to him. That idea really terrified him, because he had never been handcuffed before in his entire life. After a brief glance at the man being led away, he turned around and looked at the security officer standing next him. He was a big and tall guy. He did not look like he would smile at any time in the near future.

"Do you have any questions?" asked the officer as he handed Zvina's documents to the security officer.

"No. I don't," replied a scared and totally confused Zvina.

"If at any time you try and run away from the security officer, you will be arrested. We will detain you and send you back to Africa on the next available flight. Is that understood?" asked the officer.

"Yes," replied Zvina, nodding.

"Ok. The security officer will take you to your departure terminal," said the officer.

"Just like the officer said, I want no dirty tricks here. You follow me and do what I tell you. Let's go," said the security officer.

They left the terminal and caught a shuttle to Terminal Four. They did not speak to each other. When they arrived at Terminal Four, they passed through security and proceeded to the departure gate. They arrived at the departure gate well before the plane had started boarding. The security officer sat down on a bench and asked Zvina to sit down next to him. After sitting quietly for some time, Zvina broke the ice.

"May I use the toilet, Officer?" he asked.

"You want to use the washroom?" the officer asked in return.

"No. I don't need a bath. I just want to use the toilet," replied Zvina.

"Ok. We call them washrooms here," replied the officer with a wide grin on his face. "Come with me."

The security officer accompanied Zvina to the washroom. After using the urinal, Zvina went to the sink to wash his hands. To his surprise, there were no taps in the sinks, just pipes sticking out of the wall. He looked at the sinks on the other sides and they all looked the same. For a moment, he thought of not washing his hands, but he changed his mind after realizing that the security officer was watching him. He stood motionless for a few seconds before turning his head to see if there was someone watching him. Only the security officer was watching him.

"Just put your hands below the tap and the water will come out," said the officer, laughing.

Zvina put his hands below the tap and water started coming out. He washed his hands, and then they went back to the departure gate. After about an hour, Zvina's flight was called for boarding. Zvina thought the officer would give him his documents, but instead, the officer accompanied him to the boarding queue while still holding on to the documents. When it was Zvina's turn to have his documents checked for boarding, the officer handed the documents to the flight attendant himself. He then had a brief discussion with the flight attendant before walking away.

The flight attendant turned to Zvina and said, "Sir, please stand to the side for now. I will have to board everybody else before you."

Although Zvina did not understand what this meant, he complied. After all the other passengers had boarded, the flight attendant asked Zvina to come with her. She did not give Zvina's documents back to him. On the plane, she showed Zvina to his seat.

"You may sit down, Sir," she said. "I will not be giving you your documents. Security told me to give your documents to the flight captain. The flight captain will give you your documents when you land in Toronto."

"Ok, Madam," replied a humble and confused Zvina. He did not ask any questions because he was worried he might end up asking the wrong questions and get into trouble. He would just do whatever they told him. The flight attendant took the documents to the cockpit.

When the plane started its descent into Toronto, the flight attendant came to Zvina and told him to remain seated until all the other passengers had left the plane. Zvina waited patiently. After all the other passengers had left, the flight captain brought him his documents.

"Here are your documents, Sir. Welcome to Canada. Have a pleasant stay."

Zvina got off the plane and followed the other passengers to the baggage collection area. After picking up his baggage,

The Long Trip To Canada

he joined the queue to go through customs and immigration. When it was his turn, he walked over to the counter and handed the officer his passport. This officer was a young man probably in his mid to late twenties.

"Good evening, Sir. Where are you arriving from?" the officer asked Zvina.

"I am coming from Zimbabwe, but I just got off a flight from New York," replied Zvina.

The officer opened Zvina's passport and perused through the pages slowly. After a few minutes, he looked up and asked, "What's the purpose of your visit, Sir?"

"I am visiting my uncle," replied Zvina.

"Where does your uncle live?"

"He lives in Calgary."

"How long are you staying in Canada? Do you have a return air ticket?"

"Yes, I do. I will be in Canada for almost two months," said Zvina, as he passed his return ticket to the officer.

The officer once again took his time checking the ticket before asking, "Are you employed in Zimbabwe?"

"Yes, I am," replied Zvina.

"Why do you get two months of vacation? Can you show me proof that you are employed in Zimbabwe?"

"Sure. I have a letter from my employer as well as my last two payslips," replied Zvina.

"Can I see them, please?"

Zvina took the letter from his employer and his last two payslips and passed them to the officer.

"Ok. So how do you get two months of vacation? I don't think anyone would have that long of an annual vacation, especially at your age," the officer asked after checking the papers Zvina had given him.

"You are right. My annual vacation is only one month. The second month is leave of absence," replied Zvina.

"I see you are an engineer. How long have worked for this company?"

"Since 1996, after graduating from university."

"Ok. Do you have any ambitions of pursuing post-graduate studies in Canada?"

"No, I don't. My undergraduate degree is good enough," replied Zvina.

"Do you have another piece of ID on you? I need a second piece of ID to prove that you are the real Zvina Mawira."

"Yes, I do have my Zimbabwe national ID card," said Zvina, pulling his metal ID card from his wallet.

The officer looked at the photo on the ID, looked at Zvina, and shook his head.

"This is not you, Sir. I need your ID, not someone else's," said the officer, sounding rather irritated.

"That's my ID, Officer. That ID photo was taken when I was sixteen. I have obviously changed as I grew older over the years."

"Do you think I can believe that?"

"But Officer, look at my personal information on the ID card and on my passport. It's the same," said Zvina.

By this time, the number of travellers arriving at the customs counters was greatly reduced as it was becoming very late. The officer took Zvina's documents and went into a nearby room. He stayed in that room for almost thirty minutes. It had already been a very long day for Zvina, so he decided to sit on his baggage. He was starting to get worried.

When he saw the officer coming, he stood up and leaned over the counter, waiting to hear what he had to say.

"You said you are visiting your uncle in Calgary. Can I see your ticket to Calgary, please?" asked the officer.

"I do not have the ticket to Calgary. When I bought my ticket in Zimbabwe, my travel agent advised me that it would be cheaper to buy my ticket to Calgary when I am in Toronto,"

"Do you have the money to buy the ticket?" asked the officer.

"Yes, I do."

"Can you show me the money you are bringing into Canada?"

Zvina brought out his wallet and pulled out some U.S. dollar notes. He tried to hand them over to the officer, but he declined.

"You don't have to give me the money. I just need to know how much it is."

"It's nine hundred and sixty U.S."

"Is that all you have to spend in two months? Do you have a credit card?"

"No."

"You think you will survive in Canada for two months with only that much?" asked the officer sarcastically.

"Yes. My uncle is providing me accommodation and food. This is just pocket money," replied Zvina.

"I don't believe this. I need to search your baggage. Open your suitcase, please."

Zvina opened his suitcase and the officer searched it. After carefully going through the entire contents of the suitcase by scrutinizing one item at a time, the officer asked him to close it. It took Zvina some time to repack his belongings so that they could fit back into his suitcase. When he finished, he went back to the counter.

"Ok, Zvina. Now I need to talk to your uncle. Can you please write down your uncle's details on this piece of paper?" said the officer, handing Zvina pen and paper. "I want his full name, address, and phone number," the officer instructed.

Zvina wrote down his uncle's information and handed the pen and paper back to the officer.

"I am going to call your uncle and ask him some questions. I will be back shortly," said the officer. Then he walked into the office behind the counter.

Zvina sat back down on his suitcase and waited patiently. There was a lot going through his mind at this time. This had been and continued to be a very long and frustrating journey. He started having mixed feelings about the whole trip. He felt like asking the officer to just get him on the next flight to Zimbabwe. After about half an hour, the officer came and asked Zvina if his uncle had a cellphone.

"I don't think he has one. He would have given me the number if he had one," replied Zvina.

"We have a problem here. You uncle is not answering his home phone. He is probably not at home. I cannot let you into Canada until I speak with him and confirm what you are telling me."

"Officer, it's Friday evening. My uncle is obviously out at a pub or something. I think his invitation letter is good enough evidence to show that he is hosting me," said Zvina, trembling with anger. "I think the information I have provided is enough," Zvina repeated. "May I see your supervisor, please?"

"My supervisor will tell you the same thing. As a matter of fact, I have the authority to make the decision on my own without consulting my supervisor. Once I make that decision, my supervisor cannot overrule it," replied the officer in a forceful voice.

"Ok, then. Make the decision. I have no problem either way. I cannot give you any more information."

As Zvina and the officer were talking, another older officer approached the counter and asked, "Sean, I see you have had this gentleman here for some time. Is everything ok?"

"I had to check a few things with him," replied the officer.

"Ok. What is it?"

"He says he is visiting his uncle in Calgary. I have called his uncle several times but he is not answering his phone."

"Is that all you need to check before you let him go? Let's see his documents," said the senior officer. He picked up Zvina's documents from the counter.

The senior officer carefully looked through Zvina's documents before saying, "So you are an engineer with Anglo American Corporation in Zimbabwe?"

"Yes," replied Zvina.

"Anglo American is one of the biggest mining companies in the world. Do you like it there?"

"Yes, I do," replied Zvina.

He turned back to the other officer and said, "Sean, I think his documents are in order. You can give him a visitor's visa."

"Ok. All is good. I shall do that."

"Welcome to Canada, and have a pleasant stay," the senior officer said, shaking Zvina's hand before he left. After a few steps, he turned around and returned to the counter. "By the way, are you going to Calgary?" he asked Zvina.

"Yes, I am," replied Zvina.

"It's after midnight now. There are no more flights to Calgary today. Do you have a hotel reservation?"

"No," replied Zvina.

"You must be very tired. If you don't mind, you may go and sleep in the immigration camp. It's not very comfortable, but it's free. This will save you some money and it's better than sleeping on benches at the airport. Would you like that?" he asked.

Zvina thought for a moment. He had no idea what the camp looked like, but he liked the idea of sleeping somewhere comfortable since he was very tired.

"I do. Thank you," he replied.

"Ok. I will call the camp to send someone to pick you up. We will keep all your documents here while you go to camp. Tomorrow we will ask someone from the camp to bring you back to the airport. Then we will give you your documents and let you go," said the senior officer.

The senior officer walked away and Sean directed Zvina to sit on the bench nearby and wait. After about fifteen minutes, two security officers arrived.

"Are you Zvina Mawira?" asked one of them.

"Yes," replied Zvina.

"We are here to take you to the detention camp."

"Ok," replied Zvina.

Sean looked up at Zvina and said, "See you tomorrow. Like my supervisor said, I will ask them to bring you back here tomorrow afternoon. I will give you your documents then and you will be good to go." Sean put Zvina's documents in a drawer under the counter.

"Ok. Thank you," replied Zvina, standing up to get his luggage.

"Don't worry about your luggage, Sir. We will carry it for you," said one of the security officers. He continued, "May I have your hands, sir? I have to handcuff you."

"What? Why?" asked a perplexed Zvina.

"By law, we are supposed to handcuff you. Everybody that we take to camp with us is not in Canada legally. Therefore, we are supposed to handcuff you in case you run away from us."

The security officer handcuffed Zvina while his counterpart picked up Zvina's luggage and placed it on a trolley. One of the security officers lead Zvina while the other one pushed the trolley. They exited the building through one of the back doors and got into a vehicle that was parked right at the door. While seated in the back, Zvina could not contain his anger and frustration. He cried all the way to the camp.

When they arrived at the camp, the security officer unhandcuffed Zvina and asked him to get his luggage. They entered the building and the security officer showed Zvina to a small room that had a small single bed and no door. This is where he would spend the night. Zvina thanked the security officer and went to sleep right away. He was so tired that it did not take him long to fall asleep.

The next morning Zvina woke up around nine a.m. He quickly took a shower and went to the dining area for breakfast. After breakfast, he went back to his little room and sat on the bed reading a magazine he had picked up from the dining area. After a while, he put the magazine down and started reflecting on what had happened since he had left

Zimbabwe. He started crying again. After a few minutes, he stood up and went to watch TV in the dining area.

Late in the afternoon, two security officers handcuffed Zvina and drove him back to the airport. When they arrived at the airport, Zvina went straight to the counter where he had been the previous night. The same officer who had served him last night was behind the counter.

"Good afternoon, Zvina," the officer greeted him.

"Good afternoon, Officer."

"Ok. I am going to give you a visa for three weeks," said the officer, opening Zvina's passport.

"But Officer, I have a return ticket, and my return date is in seven weeks. Why don't you just give me seven weeks?" begged Zvina.

"You are going to have to change your return ticket. I am not going to give you a seven-week visa. You have no good reason to be in Canada for seven weeks," said the officer, stamping Zvina's passport before handing it back to him.

Zvina took his passport back, put it into his bag, and walked away. He went to an information booth nearby and asked where he could buy a ticket to Calgary. The lady at the booth showed him directions to an Air Canada ticket office. At the ticket office Zvina was very disappointed to learn that all the remaining flights to Calgary on that day had been fully booked. The earliest he could fly to Calgary was the following morning. There was nothing else he could do, so he purchased the ticket for the next morning. After buying the ticket he looked for an information booth and enquired about hotels. He found a cheap hotel that was very close to the airport. Zvina took the shuttle to the hotel. After what seemed like a very long night at the hotel, Zvina was relieved to check out. He hopped onto the shuttle back to the airport.

At the airport, Zvina quickly checked in and found his departure gate. He looked for a telephone booth so he could call his uncle and ask him to meet him at the Calgary airport. Unfortunately, his uncle could not meet him at the airport since he was working that day. He told Zvina to take a cab to his workplace. Zvina wrote down his uncle's work address and went back to sit in the Departures Lounge. Before long, he was finally on the plane to Calgary.

Chapter Six

Arrival in Calgary

Zvina arrived in Calgary on a sunny summer afternoon. He left the airport and took a cab to his uncle's workplace. When he arrived at his destination, Zvina asked the cab driver how much the bill was. He pulled out his wallet and gave the cab driver the exact amount without a tip. To his surprise, the cab driver gave him a funny look of disapproval. Zvina could not understand why. He thought the cab driver was just being rude. He got out of the cab and opened the trunk to get his luggage. This was rather strange. The cab driver did not even get out to help him take out his luggage. He thought maybe in Canada cab drivers do not help their customers take out their luggage. He took his luggage out and thanked the cab driver.

Zvina watched the cab driver drive away before turning around to look for his uncle's clothing store. He hauled his luggage up the stairs leading to the store's entrance. As he entered the store, he saw his uncle talking to a customer. Zvina could not hold back his excitement. He dropped his luggage onto the floor and ran towards his uncle, screaming with joy. His uncle turned around after hearing the screaming. He left the customer unattended and ran towards Zvina. The two men ran into each other's arms and embraced.

"How are you doing, Uncle?" said Zvina, as he released his uncle and then held him by his shoulder.

"I am fine. I am glad you are finally here. I was getting worried," replied his uncle.

"Yes. It has been quite an ordeal. At one point, I wished I could go back to Zimbabwe."

"Sandra!" said Zvina's uncle, turning back to the customer. "I am sorry I left you unattended. I just couldn't resist the joy of seeing my nephew. He has just arrived from Africa."

"Is that right?" replied the customer, walking towards Zvina and his uncle.

"Yes. Zimbabwe, Southern Africa," replied Zvina's uncle.

"Well. Welcome to Canada," said Sandra, extending her hand to greet Zvina.

"Thank you," said Zvina, as he greeted Sandra.

"Loxi! Do you come from Zimbabwe? I didn't know that," said Sandra, as she turned around to face Loxi.

"Yes, that's where I come from."

"I thought you came from Jamaica," said Sandra.

Loxi laughed before saying, "I am not surprised. You are not the only person who has said that to me. Having dreadlocks does not necessarily mean that someone comes from Jamaica. Anyone can have dreadlocks. Anyway, Zvina! Take a seat over there or take a look around the store. I will help Sandra. When I am done, I will give you a tour of the store and tell you all about it."

"Ok. I will just look around," said Zvina, turning around. He wanted to browse through the quality merchandise that was in his uncle's store.

Loxi's store was a high-end unisex clothing store. Located in a desirable part of Kensington across the Bow River from downtown Calgary, it was on a busy street surrounded by different kinds of stores, restaurants, and pubs. This was a sunny day, so it was quite busy with lots of people relaxing on restaurants and pubs patios. Back in Loxi's store, Loxi was busy with his client while Zvina walked around going from one rack of clothes to the next.

"Uncle Loxi must be doing very well," Zvina thought to himself. "If he can own a store that sells expensive clothes like these, he is definitely doing well. I can't afford a shirt in here. I like this."

After Loxi had finished with his client Sandra, he came over to Zvina and said, "Welcome again. You must be tired. I will close the store early today, so we can go home and rest."

"That's fine. Thanks, but I am not very tired. It wasn't a very long flight. Last night I went to sleep early. I must have slept for more than ten hours last night," said Zvina.

"Ok. Good to know, because we have to celebrate your arrival tonight. Anyway, let me show you around," said Loxi as he walked towards the checkout counter. "My friend and I own the store. We had this idea for years, and earlier this year we finally decided to make it happen. I quit my job at the store I was working at, in a mall south of the city, to run this store. I am the only employee. As you can see we specialize in high-end clothing only. You know your uncle;" said Loxi, patting Zvina on the shoulder, "I am da fashionista. Everybody knows me for that."

"You must be doing very well, Uncle," said Zvina.

"It's been hard since we opened the store, but I think we are slowly getting there," said Loxi.

Loxi showed Zvina around the store and the back office. He took his time showing Zvina the different expensive clothing brands they had in the store. None of the brands were manufactured locally. They were all imported from all over the world. Loxi and his friend had found a niche market for the brands they were selling. They were targeting young executives and professionals who worked for the oil and gas companies in Calgary's head offices. Loxi, being a socialite, did most of the advertising by word of mouth at social gatherings and in pubs. He was known by many who frequented Calgary's 17th Ave SW pubs. His partner also ran another business of his own.

By the time Loxi had finished showing Zvina around, it was about time to close the store. But just before he closed the store, a customer walked in.

"Hi Loxi," said the customer, walking towards Loxi and Zvina.

"Hi Shawn, my brother. How are you today?" asked Loxi, as he hugged Shawn.

"I am good, brother. And who is this?" asked Shawn, pointing at Zvina.

"Zvina is my nephew. He just arrived from Africa, Zimbabwe."

"Really? That must be a long trip. How are you doing? My name is Shawn," said Shawn, extending his hand to greet Zvina.

"I am very well, thank you," replied Zvina.

"Yeah. Welcome to Canada. When did you leave Zimbabwe?" asked Shawn.

"Last week," replied Zvina.

"Oh!" said Shawn, nodding. "So, you passed through UK and spent a few days with your other relatives there? I know Loxi has relatives in London."

"No. I went through West Africa, USA, and Toronto. I had some visa issues in Ghana that delayed my departure from there, and in Toronto, the immigration officer that served me would have sent me back to Zimbabwe if his supervisor had not intervened. By the time the supervisor asked him to give me the visa, it was late at night and there were no flights to Calgary at that time. The supervisor advised me to spend the night at the Immigration Detention Centre instead of paying for a hotel room," explained Zvina.

"I don't know why they make such a fuss about people entering Canada. I am sorry about that, my friend," said Shawn, patting Zvina on the shoulder. "I apologize on behalf of my country."

"Actually, it's not over yet. Since that immigration officer only gave me a three-week visa, I have to go to the immigration offices here to extend it. Otherwise, I will have to buy a new return ticket," said Zvina.

"What? They did not give you the eight weeks you wanted?" asked Loxi.

"No. That young officer was something else. I hope it won't be a difficult process to get an extension on my visa," said Zvina.

"My friend, if there is anything I can do to help you get your visa extension, let me know. I will be glad to help," said Shawn, looking very concerned.

"I don't know what they will require to extend the visa. Uncle Loxi, do you know what they will require to get the visa extension?" asked Zvina.

"Well, usually they want proof that you have sufficient funds to look after yourself while you are in Canada. That should not be a problem, because I can tell them that I am hosting you. All you need is your return ticket. I am taking care of your financial needs, food, and accommodation," explained Loxi reassuringly.

"Hey Loxi, I need a pair of nice dress pants and a shirt. I am going to a friend's party this weekend. Do you have anything you can recommend? You are the man, Loxi!" said Shawn, patting Loxi on his shoulder.

"Certainly, Shawn. I always have something for a handsome young man like you. Come on, I will show you a nice outfit here," said Loxi walking towards the front of the store where there were racks displaying the most expensive brands.

After a few minutes Shawn found a pair of pants and a shirt he liked. He paid for the merchandise and left the store. Loxi closed the store and they left for the transit train. While they were on the transit train, Loxi met one of his friends and introduced him to Zvina. However, they did not have a long conversation since he had to get off the train.

"Loxi, you have to bring Zvina to the Ship & Anchor tonight. We have to welcome him with some liquor shots. What time do you think you will get there?" asked the friend, as he got off the train.

"Let's make it nine," replied Loxi.

Loxi's answer surprised Zvina, because he thought nine p.m. was too late a time to start drinking. He wanted beer at that moment, and he was not going to wait until nine p.m. "The sun is still up, so nine p.m. is likely still a few hours away," he thought. He just hoped his uncle had beer at home that they could drink between now and nine o'clock. When they got to Loxi's apartment, Loxi showed him to the bedroom where he placed Zvina's luggage. The apartment was a single bedroom with an open concept kitchen and living area.

"Are you hungry, Zvina?" asked Loxi.

"A little bit, but I could use a cold beer. Do you have beer in the fridge?"

"Unfortunately, I don't," replied Loxi.

"We should have bought some on our way home. We can't just sit and not drink until nine p.m. Look at the sun; it's still up there. Nine is a few hours away," said Zvina.

Loxi started laughing. Zvina felt a little embarrassed because it seemed like he liked beer so much he could not even wait. He thought maybe in Canada people are not supposed to show their desire to drink beer like he had just done. However, he was quick to confirm his thoughts with his uncle.

"Looks like I can't wait to start drinking beer, hey? I just thought it would be too late to start drinking beer at nine p.m."

"That's not why I am laughing. Do you have a watch?"

"No. I don't."

"You have been using the sun to guess what time it is? You are not in Zimbabwe anymore, nephew. In this part of the world, in summer the days are a lot longer than the nights. Unlike Zimbabwe, here the sun does not set until ten p.m. at this time of the year. You think nine p.m. is a few hours away? It's actually eight thirty-five p.m. right now," said Loxi.

"What? You must be kidding me. All along I have been looking at the sun and thinking it was around four or five p.m. This is amazing. It's almost nine p.m. and the sun is still up there. It's like I am in a totally different world altogether," said Zvina, looking perplexed.

"It's the opposite in winter. The sun doesn't come up until nine in the morning, and it sets around four p.m.," said Loxi. "We'd better get ready to go. Would you like to take a shower first?" asked Loxi.

"I sure would, Uncle. That will make me feel a lot better," replied Zvina.

Zvina took a quick shower and they set off for the pub. Loxi's apartment was pretty close to 17th Avenue, so instead of taking a cab, they walked to the pub. On the way to the pub Loxi told Zvina all about his life in Calgary. Loxi recounted how he had moved to Calgary from Regina with his wife, and settled in Calgary. He told Zvina that he had made many friends in Calgary. Everybody seemed to like him. He was among the most popular people who frequented pubs on 17th Avenue. He even joked that if he ran for mayor of Calgary, he would win. Many people invited him to their parties such that every weekend he would normally be invited to two or three parties. He got along with people from all walks of life, rich and poor, professionals and non-professionals.

On his third day in Calgary, Zvina went to the immigration office in Calgary to have his visa extended to coincide with the return date on his ticket. He was a little worried that he might not get the extension, but to his surprise, he got the extension without any issues. Since he still had almost two months left before his return flight to Zimbabwe, Zvina considered taking some time to visit his mother and two siblings, a brother and a sister, who were living in UK. He could go to UK for a week or two, come back to Canada, and then return to Zimbabwe from Canada.

Before he left for UK, Zvina had decided that he wanted to live in Canada permanently. He really liked this country. There were lots of opportunities in the mining, oil and gas industries, which meant that it would not be very difficult for him to get a job. He did some research on the cost of living, salaries, and houses' and automobile prices. He found out that if he got a job in his field, he could have a very decent life with his family. With an average salary in his field, he could afford a good house, an average car, and be able to pay the bills comfortably. Life would be even better if Jill was working as well. He also liked the cultural diversity. Over the short time that he had been in Calgary, he had met people from all over the world.

Zvina called his wife, and after discussing it, they both agreed that immigrating to Canada would be a good move for their family. He sent his wife permanent resident application forms which she completed and sent back with all the other required documents. When Zvina received the documents, he submitted the complete application package for the three of them to the Canadian Embassy in New York. At that time Zvina also started applying for jobs in Canada. He had learned that having a job offer can speed up the application process for permanent residency. Unfortunately, Zvina did not get a job offer before leaving for the UK.

When Zvina arrived in the UK, he was given a six-month visa. As a result, his relatives in UK including his mum, persuaded him to stay in the UK for the duration of the visa. They discouraged him from going back to Zimbabwe and instead encouraged him to look for a job or apply for a postgraduate degree. He would also continue to apply for jobs in Canada. After about five months, he received an email from Cominco in Canada. They were interested in him and would schedule an interview if he was still in Canada. He did not waste time replying, and he told them that he had briefly left Canada but would be returning in a week. They scheduled an interview in two weeks.

On the day that Zvina left for Canada, he wore a new black leather jacket that he had just bought. Unfortunately, he forgot to throw away the desiccant sachet that was in the inner pocket of the jacket. The sachet got ripped somehow, and the desiccant beads came out. When Zvina was passing through customs upon arriving in Calgary, the customs officer asked to search him. When he searched the jacket pockets, he saw the desiccant beads and asked Zvina what they were.

"Those are desiccant beads. I forgot to throw away the desiccant sachet. It must have ruptured," explained Zvina.

"How do I know you are telling me the truth?" asked the officer.

"Well, as you can see, the jacket looks new. I just bought it."

"Anyone can tell me that story," said the officer, looking at Zvina directly in the eyes. "Why do you look scared?"

"I am not scared. I am just surprised that these desiccant beads are all of a sudden becoming a serious issue. You have the ripped sachet right there and it's labelled. You can tell the beads were in there," explained Zvina.

"Yes. They are a serious issue because I do not know what they are. They could be some form of a drug. Come with me," said the officer.

He took Zvina to a little room where he asked him to sit and wait. He took the desiccant beads as well as the jacket away with him. Zvina was left there sitting and wondering where this was all leading. He just prayed that he would not have to go through the same ordeal as the one he had suffered through in Toronto. He thought about the worst thing that could potentially happen to him. There was no way he would be arrested, because this was not a drug. However, they could come up with something different. Like what? They would probably ask him why he had come back to Canada again after only five months. What could he tell them? He thought for a while. Should he lie, or tell the truth? The best thing would be to tell the truth. He was here to attend an interview.

After about thirty minutes, the officer came back with Zvina's jacket.

"You can go, Sir. In future, make sure you don't travel with suspicious things on your person," said the officer as he handed Zvina's jacket back.

Zvina took his belongings and left the room. Loxi was waiting for him in the Arrivals Hall. The two men hugged, exchanged a few words, and hopped into a cab.

Over the next few days Zvina spent most of his time in Loxi's store and at the library. Those were the only two places where he could access the Internet. He wanted to research Cominco, City of Trail, and the surrounding areas. He also wanted to search for more jobs. Cominco had booked a return trip for him to Trail to attend the interview. He would fly in the afternoon and spend the night at a hotel in downtown Trail. Someone from Cominco would pick him up at the hotel and take him to the Trail Operations. They had planned a day packed with activities for him. First, he would meet the Technical Manager and after that he would attend the interview. Following the interview, he would spend the rest of the afternoon touring different plants in the Lead and Zinc Operations. He couldn't wait for that day.

It was a chilly late morning when Loxi's friend picked Zvina up and drove him to the airport. He was quick to check-in and then he found his departure gate. Before long, he was on a little aircraft buzzing high over the Rocky Mountains on his way to Castlegar. When they landed in Castlegar, the time was exactly the same as when they had left Calgary. Zvina thought the clock was wrong, so he asked the lady at the information desk. The clock was right. This confused Zvina.

"You look confused, Sir. Can I help in any way?" asked the lady at the information desk.

"Yes. This is not making sense to me. We left Calgary an hour ago, and we flew for exactly an hour. But you are telling me that the time here is the same as the time I left Calgary."

"Oh yes, Sir. Calgary is one hour ahead of us. You gained an hour coming here," said the lady at the information desk.

"Ok," said Zvina, beating his forehead with his palm, "I had totally forgotten that. In fact, I thought there was no time difference since it's just a short distance between Calgary and Castlegar. Anyway, thank you very much."

Zvina turned around and found his way out of the airport terminal building. He got into a waiting cab and was soon on his way to Trail. After checking in at the hotel, he went to his room and watched TV. Just before dinner, he got a call from reception. Someone from Cominco wanted to meet him in the lobby. He went down and met a man who introduced himself as the technical manager. He asked Zvina to come with him for a ride around the city of Trail and surrounding areas. After the drive, they had dinner together at the hotel before the technical manager left.

The following morning a young engineer picked up Zvina and took him to the administration building where the technical manager's office was. The technical manager introduced him to many employees there, including other engineers. Sometime mid-morning, the interview was conducted. The technical manager and two other managers sat in on the interview. It was a very long interview, but Zvina had a good feeling about this job. When he left the interview, an engineer from lead operations was waiting to take him on a tour of the Lead Operations. Zvina was pleased by what he saw. He thought this would be a great plant to work at. After the Lead Operations tour, they had lunch with three other engineers. After lunch, one of the other engineers took Zvina on a tour of the Zinc Operations. Once again, Zvina was pleased by what he saw.

Unlike the smelter where Zvina had worked in Zimbabwe which produced two alloys only, ferrochrome and ferrosilicon chrome, this operation produced a number of pure metals including gold and silver and other chemicals. It was an integrated operation with several metallurgical extraction processes including smelting, roasting, leaching, electrowinning, and refining, just to name the big ones. A young engineer like Zvina would never be short of challenges working at an operation like this.

Back at the main administration building, Zvina was shown back into the interview room. The three gentlemen who had interviewed him in the morning were all there.

"Well, Zvina," the technical manager broke the ice, "how were the tours?"

"They were very good, thank you. You have a great operation here. It's indeed a world class operation," replied Zvina.

"It's certainly one of the biggest integrated lead-zinc operations in the world. Unfortunately, time is not on our side. You could have visited the other small operations," said one of the other managers.

"You have to catch your flight back to Calgary in one-and-a-half hours. Let's get down to business, so we can let you go," said the technical manager.

"The three of us here think that the interview went very well this morning," said the other manager. "Therefore, we are recommending hiring you."

Zvina could not believe his ears. He just stared at the three men sitting in front of him and could not say a word. His mouth was wide open.

"Are you excited?" asked the technical manager.

"I am very excited. I don't know what to say," said Zvina.

"Let's talk about next steps. HR is going to contact you to get things going. Basically, they are going to engage an immigration lawyer who will work with you to process a work permit. Once you have the work permit, you may join us here at Trail Operations. You will be a process engineer in Lead Operations. Congratulations!" said the technical manager, as he stood up to give Zvina a handshake.

The other two managers also stood up and gave Zvina handshakes. They had a short informal discussion during which they asked Zvina about his personal life including his family and interests. After that, they bade him farewell and he went back to Castlegar to catch the plane back to Calgary. On the plane, he thought about a new life in Canada. He also thought about working at the Trail Operations. He had always dreamed of working at such a big metallurgical complex, but it had never dawned on him that that dream would come true. This was just unbelievable.

The following week, the immigration lawyer that Cominco had hired to assist in the work permit application process contacted Zvina. He told Zvina that he had to go back to Zimbabwe since the application would be processed at the Canadian Embassy in South Africa. The Canadian Embassy in Zimbabwe did not process work permit applications. The necessary medical examinations would have to be done in the home country as well. So, Zvina left Canada and went back to UK where he stayed with his mother for a few weeks before proceeding to Zimbabwe.

Chapter Seven

Work Permit Application

When the plane landed at Harare International Airport, Zvina could hardly contain his excitement. He had been gone for over eight months. This was the longest time he had ever been away from Zimbabwe. His son had just turned one when he had left. He wondered if his son would still remember him. The queues at Immigration and Customs moved fast, and within thirty minutes, Zvina was in the Arrivals Hall where his wife, son, relatives, and friends were waiting. He picked up his son first before greeting anyone else. His son was calm. He looked puzzled.

"Hi, sonny boy! Do you remember me? It's Dad. I am your dad."

"I think he remembers you. He is just puzzled right now. Obviously, he did not expect to see you," Jill explained.

"I wonder what's going on in his mind. He must be thinking, 'Where the heck have you been?' He doesn't look like he is going to say a word," said Zvina.

After hugging his wife, Zvina turned around and started greeting the other people who had accompanied his family to the airport. Munya and Tindo were also there. They had both moved to Bulawayo, the country's second largest city, after they were transferred by their companies. They had come to see their friend on his arrival.

"Munya! Tindo!" shouted Zvina. He shook hands with his friends, and asked, "When did you guys get here?"

"We left Bulawayo early in the morning. The highway was not very busy," replied Munya.

"How was your flight?" asked Tindo.

"It was good, but I am tired. Let's go home, everybody," said Zvina, getting back to his wife.

The whole party of people split into three groups. Each group got into one of the three cars that were there and they all drove home.

When they got home, there was a mini gathering already. Friends and relatives had come to see Zvina.

Although Zvina was tired, he did not take a nap at any time that afternoon. He could not wait to get updated on what was going on in the country. The fuel situation had improved slightly, but the economy had continued to rapidly decline. The rate of inflation was close to one hundred percent. Some industries were shutting down, and a lot of workers had been sent into the streets. The agricultural sector, which used to be the backbone of the economy, was almost non-existent. The commercial farms had been ceased by Zanu-PF's supporters in a land distribution revolution that was championed by the war veterans. The low gold price, at less than three hundred U.S. dollars in 2001, was not helping the economy. This had led to some gold mine closures in Zimbabwe's once thriving gold mining industry. With so many people losing their jobs, the informal sector was on the rise. In the high-density areas, many people were opening up little tuck shops in their front yards where they sold anything from cigarettes to clothes. In the back yards, little structures, which people called cottages, were sprouting up. They were becoming a major source of rental income for those that had big back yards. While some of these structures were well-built, others were literally shacks made from corrugated iron sheets and plastic. In the central business district, young men loitered around the streets with huge bundles of local currency notes which they sold for U.S. dollars and South African rands. Their exchange rates went up daily.

"My friend it's a dog's breakfast here," said Tindo, winding down his long narration of what was going on in the country.

"It's so sad," said Zvina. "Other countries are progressing, yet we are going down."

"All the more reason to leave," Munya reasoned. "You are moving in the right direction. I never thought things would get this bad."

"Tell me: how is Bulawayo?" asked Zvina.

"It's not very different," replied Munya. "The only differences are that the pace of life in Bulawayo is a bit slower, and over the years a lot of Bulawayans have moved to work in South Africa. Those people bring money back into the city. So, things are a little cheaper. The black-market exchange rate for the rand is lower in Bulawayo than in Harare."

"Just to show you how desperate people are," Tindo interjected, "some people are buying rands in Bulawayo and coming to sell them in Harare. People are just doing whatever they can to make a living."

"You must be kidding me! Really?" said Zvina, with compassion.

"Anyway, I prefer Bulawayo to Harare," said Munya. "What do you think, Tindo?"

"I am with you, Munya. I like Bulawayo better," said Tindo. Then he asked Zvina, "So, what's your plan?"

"After what you guys have just told me, I can't wait to leave this country," replied Zvina. "As I told you before, I got a job offer in Canada. I will be submitting a work permit application at the Canadian Embassy in South Africa. Once I get the permit, I will be out of here."

"Ok. How long will that take?" asked Munya.

"I have no idea. I will find out once I start the process. I think it will take at least three months, based on my research," replied Zvina.

"You should come and visit us in Bulawayo before you go. We will take you to some good pubs," said Tindo.

"What pubs?" asked Zvina, laughing. "You mean shebeens? I know there are a lot of shebeens in Bulawayo. Ndebele women are very good at running shebeens."

"No, we don't do shebeens. There are some good pubs downtown," said Munya.

"I will see. I will be bored here without you guys," said Zvina.

By the time Zvina went to bed, he had a good picture of the situation in Zimbabwe. He was determined to leave the country at his earliest opportunity.

While Zvina had been away, his wife had applied for a job with a UK–based company that was recruiting pharmacists in Southern Africa for positions in the UK. She got the job, and the company had started the work permit application

The Long Trip To Canada

process for her. This was something that Zvina and his wife had to discuss, since Zvina would be applying for a work permit in Canada. On his second day after arrival, when his wife returned home after work, they started the discussion.

"Honey, since you have applied for a UK work permit and I will be applying for a Canadian work permit, I think we should discuss this. We can't live in different countries. We must choose one of the two," said Zvina.

"Yes. We have always preferred Canada. I think we should stick to that," said Jill.

"I think so too. For me, being in the mining industry, Canada is a better choice. There isn't much mining happening in the UK anymore," commented Zvina.

"Do you think I should cancel my application for the UK work permit?" asked Jill.

"No. You don't have to. You never know. Something might happen with my application and it may not get approved. If you cancel your application, and then my application doesn't get approved for whatever reason, we will have lost both opportunities," reasoned Zvina.

"I see your point. Let's just have the two applications processed. Hopefully, yours gets approved sooner than mine. Then we can cancel my application and go to Canada. I wish this job offer was in Canada. I have applied for jobs in Canada, but I have not gotten any response. Maybe they want people to be registered with their College of Pharmacists before being considered for employment," said Jill.

"I think that's the way to go," Zvina agreed. Then Jill thought of a possible obstacle to their plan. "Sometimes in the application forms they ask if the applicant has similar applications pending elsewhere. I hope they won't ask that in your application. If they do, I hope my application won't affect yours."

"I hope not. But that should not be a problem. Although we are married, we are still two different individuals and our applications should be seen as such."

"You are right. I don't think we need to worry about that. Let's keep both applications going."

A week after Zvina had arrived in Zimbabwe, the immigration lawyer contacted him and told him that he was sending the work permit application package to him by courier. After a few days, Zvina received the package. He reviewed the package with his wife and started gathering together all of the required documentation.

Zvina needed a police clearance report as well. When he went to get the police clearance report, he was shocked to discover that he had a reckless driving conviction on record. He had never been convicted of reckless driving. He had been summoned to appear in court with reckless driving charges a few years back, but the charges had been dropped before he was tried.

"Officer, I am surprised that I have a conviction record in my file. I was never convicted of reckless driving. This entry must be a mistake."

"That's a minor conviction. I would not worry about that," replied the officer.

"Well, it doesn't matter whether it's minor or not. I have never been convicted. So that should not be on my record."

"I cannot help you. I only retrieve what's on record. If you want that removed, you will have to go back to the court where the entry was made and get it corrected there. It shows that the entry was made at the Shurugwi Magistrates Court.

That's where you should go to have this corrected. What do you need the police clearance for? This is not a major conviction; most organizations do not even look at such convictions. If I were you, I would just leave it there because it's more of a hassle to remove it. No one will crucify you for such a petty conviction."

"I need it for a work permit application in Canada."

"What type of work?"

"I am an engineer."

The officer started laughing.

"So why are you worried about a reckless driving conviction on your record? You are not going to work as a driver in Canada. So why would this be an issue?"

"I see what you mean, Officer, but I will obviously be driving on their roads. No one would want reckless drivers on their roads."

"Ok, my friend. It's up to you. I have told you what you need to do if you want to have this record removed."

"I have to think about this. Anyway, I will take the report. Thank you."

Zvina took the report and left. When he got home he told his wife about the conviction record on his police clearance report. They discussed the issue at length and finally decided that Zvina had to go to Shurugwi to have the record corrected. They did not want anything that would potentially jeopardize the work permit application. The next day, Zvina went to Shurugwi and got the record corrected. Since the record system was manual, it would take some time for the record to be updated. The magistrate at Shurugwi Court gave Zvina a letter to take back to the CID HQ in Harare. This would give the officers at CID HQ the authority to delete the reckless driving record from Zvina's file.

When Zvina finally got his police clearance report, he had all the documentation required for his application. He couriered the package to the immigration lawyer in Canada. The lawyer would submit the application package to the Canadian Embassy in South Africa on his behalf.

Two months went by and neither Zvina nor his wife heard from the immigration office where they had submitted their work permit application. This waiting period seemed like decades for Zvina, as he was not working at that time. During the week, Zvina would sleep in. When he got up, he would spend a few hours playing with his son until mid-afternoon. Then he would go downtown and have a few drinks while waiting for his wife to finish work. After work, Jill would join him for a drink or two before they went home. This became a daily routine for a few months. On weekends, they would visit relatives or invite friends and relatives over for barbeque and drinks. They wanted to make the best of the time they had left in Zimbabwe, because they were certain that at least one of their applications would come through soon. Although they preferred Canada, at that time in their lives, they simply wanted a fresh start. Zvina could not wait to get back to work, but he did not want to go back to work in Zimbabwe.

Jill's application finally got approved and she submitted her passport for the visa. In less than two weeks, she received the passport back with the visa. At that time, her new employer started making travel arrangements for her. They wanted her to start work in UK in two months. This was another decision-making point for Zvina and Jill. Should they decline the UK offer and wait for the Canadian work permit? If they declined this offer, then what if the Canadian work permit application was rejected? They would lose both opportunities. But what would they do if Jill took the UK offer and the Canadian work application got approved? Would she be legally bound in an agreement to work for this employer for the full contract term? Zvina and Jill did not want to live in different countries.

"My new employer wants me to start work in UK in two months. They want to make travel arrangements for me now. Should I just let them go ahead?" Jill asked her husband one evening after going through the pack of mail they had received that day.

"Just let them go ahead. Like we said before, the Canadian work permit is not one hundred percent guaranteed. Anything can happen and we may fail to get it. This bird we have in the hand is worth more than two in the jungle. Let's for go for it. We can always deal with the situation when it arises. I mean if I get the Canadian work permit, we will see what we can do depending on what's happening at the time. The worst-case scenario is that we live separately for some time, but we will be working on getting you and Fari to join me in Canada."

"My work permit is for three years. I will look at the contract again to see if I will be penalized if I decided to leave before the contract expires."

"Good point. We need to know if you will be penalized if you quit and what that penalty is."

"I will check."

"I know there are some Canadian pharmacy chains recruiting pharmacists from overseas as well. Remember the ad I told you I saw in the UK? You can also find out if your new employer has a Canadian affiliate that is recruiting. You could request a transfer to the Canadian affiliate."

"That's a possibility. I will look into this too. Do you still remember the name of the Canadian company that was recruiting in UK?"

"I can't remember off the top of my head right now, but I wrote it down in my notebook. I will find it for you."

"This is a very confusing situation," said Jill with a frustrated laugh. "I wish the Canadian work permit application was guaranteed. Then we wouldn't have to go through all of this uncertainty."

"You are right. It's been a few months now, and we haven't heard from them. That kind of worries me."

"The application package said that at some point during the process, we all have to go for medicals. What's going to happen if I leave for the UK before we do the medicals?"

"I don't know. I guess we could ask them if you can do your medicals in the UK."

"I don't think they will allow that. Remember, they said that your application has to be processed in your home country or at an Embassy nearest to your home country if the Canadian Embassy in your home country does not process the applications."

"This makes it tricky for us, because we can't afford to fly you back for the medicals. Besides, you might not have accumulated enough vacation time to be able to take time to fly back," Zvina pointed out.

"You are right. But I will check their vacation terms and conditions to confirm," Jill assured him.

"You know what? I may have to drop you from the application," said Zvina, looking very frustrated and confused.

"But putting in that request will slow your permit application process. And I think they will require documentation from me as proof that I have given you the authority to take the kid to Canada."

"Another complication," sighed Zvina.

"You know, this idea of me going to the UK and leaving you guys here is bugging me. I can't afford to stay in the UK alone for an indefinite time period before you guys join me. If the Canadian work permit does not come out by the time I go to the UK, you guys have to follow right after."

"I hear you. I also can't wait to leave this country. I am sick and tired of being a loafer. I need to go back to work. I agree with you. I think we should follow you right after. At least I can look for a job in UK and start working."

"That's what we will do. I will let my new employer know that I am ready to travel to UK as planned."

"Yes, go ahead. I pray and hope that we can at least get the medicals done before you leave. That will make our lives a lot easier," said Zvina as he stood up. "This is very stressful. I need a beer."

"I see this is stressing you out very much. I think you need to relax and take it easy. Things will work out. I bet your blood pressure is high these days because of this. This is not worth dying for. Besides, the application has not been rejected. It's just a slow process."

Zvina went into the kitchen, got a beer, and went outside to join his cousin who was sitting on the veranda of their rental cottage. Jill stood up and took the mail to their bedroom.

A few days later, Zvina and Jill were relieved to receive a package from Canadian Immigration with information on the required medical examinations. They did not waste time. They booked appointments and had the medicals done within a week.

As the time for Jill's departure to UK drew closer, things took a complete turnaround for Zvina. In the months since he had returned from overseas, time had seemed to drag along very slowly. Days had felt like months, weeks had felt like years, and months had felt like decades. In sharp contrast, as the countdown for Jill's departure rolled along, days felt like hours and weeks felt like days. Zvina hoped that they would hear from Canadian Immigration before his wife left. Every day, he would make sure he was the first person to get to the mailbox. To his disappointment, they received nothing from the Canadian Embassy. This affected Zvina so much that within two weeks, it was evident that he was losing weight. One day, his uncle invited him to a pub downtown and sat him down to discuss his situation.

"Young man, we all know that you are trying to get out of this country, but things are not working out as you wish," his uncle began after taking a sip from a frosty chilled glass of beer.

"I know."

"Yes. We can all see that it's wreaking havoc on you and your health. Do you realize that?"

"Yes, I do."

"Do you think that going to Canada or the UK is more important than your health or life?"

"No. Not at all."

"So, be a man. Be strong. In life, nothing comes easy. If going to live and work in Canada and the UK was easy, most of us wouldn't be here. It's not easy. That's why most of us can't even apply for work permits to go and work there. So be thankful and be happy that at least you meet some of the requirements, if not all. Be grateful that you have an application in progress. In fact, instead of worrying over this, you should be singing 'Jesus is wonderful' all the time as you wait for your work permit to come through. I don't think the gods will be pleased if you continue to worry over this. This is affecting your wife and kid. This is now also affecting your father, your mother, and your grandmother too. This is affecting everybody who loves you. We cannot watch you continue down this path."

"I wasn't aware that I thought about it that much, but I guess I do subconsciously. I can't get it out of my mind."

"The problem is not getting it out of your mind. The problem is that you think that the outcome may not be what you want. That's what you need to get out of your mind. Everything is going to be fine. You will get the permit and you will go and live and work in Canada. Even if your wife has to go to the UK for some time, she will eventually join you. Even if you do not get the work permit, you can go and live in the UK. Not living in Canada is not the end of life. Now I want you to get that negative thinking out of your mind. Everything is going to be fine. Enjoy the last few days with your wife here in Zimbabwe before she leaves. Visit as many of her relatives as you can with her and bid them all farewell. Tell them that you will be joining her shortly after."

"Ok. I will do as you say, Uncle."

Zvina and his uncle continued to discuss other family issues until two of his friends, Tindo and Munya, joined them in the pub. Tindo and Munya had just arrived from Bulawayo. They wanted to spend the day with Zvina before proceeding to Marondera to visit Munya's parents.

"How are you doing, old man?" said Tindo as he shook Uncle Dino's hand.

"And how are you doing, young man?" said Munya, shaking hands with Zvina.

After exchanging greetings, the two newcomers ordered their beers and joined in the conversation.

"Uncle D, you need to talk to our poor buddy Zvina. This work permit application thing seems to be chewing him up. He is getting worse every day, for that matter. He should not stress over it."

"You are right, Tindo," echoed Munya.

"You are both right. That's what we were discussing before you got here. He's working on it," said Uncle Dino.

Zvina reassured the group, "You are all right. Like Uncle D said before you guys got here, I have been filled with negative thoughts. I have been wondering what I would do if the permit application is rejected. I have allowed myself to just sink into an emotional rut because if this. But it is what it is. Whether I get the work permit or not, life goes on. I will not die because I couldn't get a Canadian work permit. On the other hand, there is really no reason why I should think that the application will be rejected. I shouldn't really dwell on the negative here. Thanks for putting me in the right mindset. I bet I will be a changed man going forward."

The four dropped the subject and talked about a lot of other things before they retired for the night. Munya gave Zvina a ride back home.

Two weeks prior to Jill's departure, Jill and Zvina had to decide what to do with their household property. One evening after dinner, Jill started the conversation.

"What are we going to do with our household stuff?"

"I think we should sell most of it. We can give away the smaller and older items," replied Zvina.

"Like what?"

"I think the stove, fridge, sofas, bedroom suite, and TV should be sold. Everything else can be given away."

"You know *the everything else* you are talking about is the kitchen utensils? Those can only be given to my people, not yours. Do you know that?"

"I know that. It's tradition. I don't want my kids to be in trouble when you are gone. Whatever is yours should be given to your relatives now."

"We are going to have to advertise the other things in the paper. We should do that this week. We only have two weeks to go. When I leave, you guys will have to move out and stay with Gogo until you come to join me in the UK."

"We can advertise, but I think we should tell our relatives and friends first. Some of them might want to buy the stuff. I would feel bad if a relative or friend said we should have told them about the stuff we are selling after the stuff is all sold. I will tell as many friends and relatives as possible and you do the same. Then we will advertise at the beginning of next week," said Zvina, getting up to go and get a beer from the fridge. "Do you want a glass of wine?"

"No, thank you. Give me Amarula instead. With milk and ice," said Jill, pausing momentarily before continuing, "Will the buyers collect the stuff right away? We need these things until our move out day."

"You are right. I think we should ask them to pick up the stuff on our move out day. They can pay a security deposit, say twenty-five percent to secure their purchase, and then pay the balance when they come to pick up the stuff," said Zvina, handing Jill a glass of Amarula with milk and ice.

"Good idea. Let's do that," said Jill, accepting the glass.

"I don't think we should sell the two beds and the wardrobes. We will give one bed and wardrobe to Simo, since we are going to rent him a room in Harare while he finishes his diploma at Harare Polytechnic. We will send the bed and wardrobe from our bedroom to our rural home. One of the bedrooms there doesn't have a bed in it," suggested Zvina. After opening his bottle of Castle Lager, he sat down. He gulped down the beer from the bottle before placing it on the coffee table.

"I LOVE this beer," he said, smiling at his wife. "Have you decided who you will give your kitchen stuff to?"

"The most appropriate recipients are my sisters. But both of my sisters are still young and single. They don't have households of their own, so I can't give them my kitchen stuff. I will have to give them to my married cousin Vari. She is the only close sister who is married and has her own household. I could also just put them into storage and keep them there until we come back to live in Zimbabwe, or until my two sisters have their own households."

"Not a good idea. I think you should just give them away. You never know how long it's going to be before we come

The Long Trip To Canada

back to live in Zimbabwe, and at that time you will definitely have better kitchen stuff from overseas. You won't like these things anymore. As for your sisters, again you never know. They might go overseas as well."

"I will think about it."

In the following days, they told their friends and relatives about what they were selling. By the end of that week, everything had been sold except for the sofas. They advertised the sofas in the local newspaper and they were sold on the first day the advertisement was published.

Jill's last day at work was a week before she left for the UK. They had decided that they would use that last week to travel and visit close relatives. This way Jill would have the opportunity to bid them farewell. Their first trip was to Bocha, Zvina's rural homeland. His father and stepmother lived there. They borrowed a car from Jill's aunt and drove to Bocha. Jeni (Jill's sister), Fari, and Simo came along. It was a three-hour drive to Mutare, and by the time they got there, Fari was restless and crying. They stopped at Nandos for lunch. After lunch, they bought some groceries to take to their rural home. It is customary in Zimbabwe to always bring some groceries for the rural folks when coming from the city. They also bought some beers which Zvina and Simo drank on their way to Bocha.

When they arrived at the rural homestead, Zvina's dad, Sekuru, was home. He was very happy to see them and welcomed them into the house.

"No, Baba, I would rather we sit outside," said Zvina. "It is very hot inside."

"Ok. Get yourselves stools," said Sekuru.

They all sat down and exchanged greetings. At that time, Zvina's stepmother arrived. She was carrying a bucket of water on her head. She had gone to fetch water from the local communal well which was about half a kilometre from their homestead. She went into the round hut (kitchen) to put the bucket away before coming to join everybody outside. After the greetings, the women went into the kitchen to prepare supper. The men stayed behind and continued their conversations. Zvina told his dad the reason for their visit. His wife was going to the UK and he would stay behind with their son. They would join his wife in a few weeks after she was settled.

"I hear what you are saying, son, but this worries me. You should be the one going first, and then, once you are settled, she and your son would follow. You are the man, so you are supposed to take the lead in such endeavours," said Sekuru, rubbing his long white beard with his right hand.

"I know, Baba, but this is different. For anyone to go there like she is doing, they ought to have a job there first. I don't have a job there, so I can't go. She was lucky to get a job, so she can go. The kid and I are actually relying on her to get permission for us all to live in the UK."

"You could all go at the same time then," said Sekuru.

"We can't, Baba. When she gets there, she will be in training for two weeks and they will have her staying in a hotel. They won't allow us to stay in the hotel with her."

"Such things are not allowed in our tradition. I hope you will follow her as soon as possible," said Sekuru, looking very concerned.

The family stayed up late that night. They had a lot to discuss before Jill left. Sekuru gave Jill and Zvina a lot of advice. He particularly emphasized that Zvina and Fari join Jill as soon as possible. He did not want the couple to be separated for too long.

The next day Zvina and his company left for Harare. They spent the night in Harare and the next morning they left for Madziva. Jill's grandmother lived in Madziva. She had raised Jill. She was like Jill's mother, so Jill had to go and see her before she left. When they arrived at the homestead in Madziva, Jill's grandmother, Ambuya, was busy watering her vegetables in her little garden by the homestead. On seeing the car pull up to the house, she left what she was doing and came over.

"Welcome! Welcome," said Ambuya, greeting her visitors.

"We are here, Ambuya," said Zvina, getting out of the car.

"What are you doing in the garden in this hot weather?" asked Jill, as she hugged Ambuya.

"I have to water my vegetables or else they will dry up and die. It's too hot," said Ambuya. "Let's go inside."

"No, Ambuya. Let's sit on the veranda. It's hot inside," said Jill.

"You are right. Sometimes there is a cool breeze on the veranda," said Ambuya.

They all sat on the veranda and exchanged greetings. After a while, Zvina and Simo excused themselves.

"Ambuya, we are going to the stores to while up time with brother-in-law Biri and his friends. Shall we bring you some drinks when we come back?" said Zvina.

"You don't have to ask that. In fact, it will be too late if we have to wait until you come back. Please send someone back with the drinks right away. We are thirsty," Jill interjected.

"Ok. Will do. Simo! Let's go," said Zvina.

The next morning, while they were getting ready to leave Madziva, Ambuya sat Zvina and Jill down.

"Jill tells me that she is leaving for the UK on Saturday," Ambuya began.

"Yes," replied Zvina.

"When are you and Fari following her?"

"We are not sure of the exact dates yet, but as soon as she is settled."

"Ok. You must make sure that you follow her as soon as possible. It worries us to have young couples like you staying apart from each other. There are bad things out there. Temptations, diseases, you name it. We don't want to lose you and we don't want you to lose each other."

"You are right, Ambuya. We will make sure we join her in the UK as soon as possible."

"Who will look after Fari when Jill is gone?"

"Jeni will look after him," replied Jill. "She is very good with kids, and Fari likes her."

"That's alright. I will have to talk to her as well. These young girls need some advice. She must know when to feed the child, check his diapers, and bathe him. She can be playful sometimes. Have you been to Bocha to say farewell to your father-in-law?"

"Yes, Ambuya. We came back from there the day before yesterday," said Jill.

"How about your aunties and uncles? You must make sure you visit them all and say goodbye. That's what you are supposed to do in our tradition."

"We will do that, Ambuya."

"And when you get overseas, don't forget us. Call us from time to time. Come back home from time to time."

"For sure, Ambuya. We will come back to see you every year."

"Good! You must also buy your own house in Harare. At some point in your lives, you will want to come back home. Don't be like some people we have seen. They lived overseas for years and when they came back home, they were destitutes. The world will laugh at you," Ambuya advised Jill and Zvina.

"Goodbye, Ambuya. Let me know when you go to Harare or to the farm, so I can call and talk to you. I wish you had a phone line here," said Jill, wiping tears from her cheeks.

"Don't worry, my child. I will be ok here. Each time I visit the girls in Harare, I will ask them to let you know so that you can call," said Ambuya, hugging Jill.

"Mukanya, please come back and see me before you follow her," said Ambuya, shaking hands with Zvina.

"Ok, Ambuya. Once we know the actual departure date, we will come and see you," replied Zvina.

Zvina and his party got into the car and left. They passed through Jill's uncle's farm and bade Jill's auntie and cousins farewell. They also passed through Zvina's sister's place before proceeding back to Harare.

On the day before Jill's departure, Zvina's family packed up everything and the people who had bought the furniture came to pick up their merchandise. They moved everything they were keeping to Jill's auntie's house. When the cottage was empty, they cleaned it and called their landlord to inspect it. The landlord was happy and asked Zvina to come back the next day to collect their damage deposit. Zvina packed the rest of their remaining belongings before they left.

That was the beginning of a new life. On the way to Westwood, there was very little conversation between Zvina and Jill. They were both lost in their thoughts. They both wondered what the future had in store for them.

When they arrived in Westwood they were surprised to find a number of their relatives' cars parked outside the gate and the driveway. They had not expected them to come on this day. They had expected them to come on the following day to see Jill off to the airport. However, their relatives had arranged a farewell party for Jill that evening. Most of their friends and relatives who lived in Harare were there. Most men were seated outside, enjoying their beer. Some women were preparing food, while others were busy gossiping in the living room. Loud bursts of laughter were heard every few moments. A large barbeque was going on close to where the men were seated. From time to time the man behind the barbeque would pass a plate full of barbequed meat around to the men. Zvina and Simo joined the men while Jill and Jeni joined the women in the living room. Fari went straight to the barbeque and asked for meat.

"Ndoda nyama (I want meat)," he demanded.

"Zvina," shouted one of the men, "look at your son. He likes meat like you. Like father, like son. I bet he already drinks beer too, just like you."

"Yes, he likes meat like me, but not beer. He says it's bitter, so he doesn't like it," replied Zvina.

"I know why," another man jumped in, "you always take him kwaMereki."

"He doesn't want to stay home. Each time someone leaves home, he wants to go with them, especially me," said Zvina. "Sometimes he just gets the car keys and says, 'Dad, let's go.'

If I have to leave home without him, I have to sneak out or ask his nanny to go for a walk with him."

By mid-evening, many relatives and friends had gathered. There was lots of food and drink. A local DJ had joined and was playing his disco. Some people danced to the music, while others stood or sat in groups chatting. Jill was like a little heroine that evening. Everybody wanted to have the opportunity to talk to her. The attention that Jill was getting kind of disturbed Fari. He sensed there was something happening with his mother. He clung to his mum the whole evening, even beyond his normal bedtime. A number of people had offered to take him, but he wouldn't leave his mum.

By late evening, the gathering had turned into a big party. The DJ was playing his disco full blast. Lots of people had now come onto the dance floor. There was lots of beer and soft drinks, and the barbeque was still churning out lots of meat. The party continued past midnight. Jill left for bed around midnight, but Zvina stuck around. He went to sleep after everybody had left.

The following morning, Jill woke up very early to pack her luggage. Everybody else woke up late except the housemaid. She helped Jill with her ironing before starting her daily chores. After Jill finished packing, she woke Zvina up. They were supposed to go and have breakfast at Zvina's grandmother's house in Greendale. They had quick showers and left for Greendale. By the time they got back from Greendale, it was time to leave for the airport. The whole family and some friends accompanied them to the airport.

From the time they left the house for the airport, Fari clung to his mum. He appeared to have sensed that his mum was leaving. Other people including Jeni tried to take him away from his mum, but Fari refused. Zvina and Jeni knew that it would be difficult to separate Fari from his mum at the airport. They had to find a way to get him distracted somehow when his mum left. Zvina remained calm. He knew he had to be strong because if he broke down, that would affect Jill who was already battling with her own emotions. She managed to suppress her emotions by talking all the time.

After Jill had checked in, it was time to bid everyone farewell. Zvina persuaded Fari to let him be taken from Jill. At first, he refused; but after a few trials, Zvina managed to win Fari over. Jill then went on to bid everyone farewell before coming back to Zvina and Fari. They knew that if Fari saw Jill disappear into the Departures Lounge, he would cry. So, after kissing Jill, Zvina told Fari that they were going to get some drinks in the restaurant. After Zvina and Fari had left, Jill bade farewell to everyone again and disappeared into the Departures Lounge.

Several days passed, and Zvina had still not heard anything from the Canadian Embassy. One afternoon while he was reading a book on the veranda, the postman stopped by with some letters. Zvina accepted the letters and quickly scanned through them. There was a letter from the Canadian Embassy, which he quickly opened and started reading. To his disappointment, the Embassy wanted him to do more medical examinations. He called the medical centre right away and made an appointment. He was lucky to get an appointment on the next day. After he got off the phone, he started thinking. What were these further examinations? Why were they required? Was this something that could potentially jeopardize his visa application? The more he thought about it, the more worried he became. He put the letters and the book he was reading in the house and went for a walk.

The following day, he drove his aunt to work and went to the medical centre for his further examinations. At the medical centre, he checked in and sat down in the waiting room. After a few minutes, he was called up into the doctor's examination room.

"Hello, Zvina," the doctor greeted Zvina as he walked in. "Take a seat."

"Hello, Doctor. How are you?" replied Zvina.

"Very well, thank you. How are you?"

"I am fine. Thank you."

"I see the Canadians want us to do more tests on you."

"Yes. What are these tests for? I thought we did everything last time."

"Yes, but when we did the tests, your blood pressure was very high. It's nothing serious. They just want to confirm that you do not have a heart problem. We will do an ECG one more time. Then we will give you a blood pressure monitor that you must keep on you for twenty-four hours. It will measure and record your blood pressure every hour. We will also give you a two-litre bottle to collect a urine sample. Again, collect the urine sample into the bottle for twenty-four hours. Ok?"

"Wow! That's quite a task, Doctor," said Zvina, with a plastic smile.

"I know. Unfortunately, that's what we have to do. I don't think it's a show stopper. I have examined you before and I am confident your high blood pressure last time was just a one-off incident caused by anxiety or something."

"I hope so."

"Ok. Let's get the ECG done and we will get the other stuff ready for you."

After the ECG, the nurse put the blood pressure monitor on Zvina's arm and told him not to remove it for the next twenty-four hours. She also gave him the urine sample bottle to take with him. From the medical centre, Zvina went back home and spent the rest of the day relaxing and watching TV. He did not want to be involved in any physical activities since he had the blood pressure monitor on him. The next morning, he went back to the medical centre and had the blood pressure monitor taken off. He also returned the two-litre bottle which was almost completely full of his urine sample. As he left the medical centre, Zvina thought about the past twenty-four hours. Although they were not physically or emotionally painful, they had certainly been unusual. Urinating in a bottle for twenty-four hours and having the blood pressure monitor squeezing his arm every hour was quite a life experience. He hoped it would never happen again. He did not have a good sleep that night.

After Jill had completed her orientation and training, she was deployed to Sheffield. She moved into a B&B for a few days before finding a place to rent. At that time, she sent Zvina all the necessary information, so that he could apply for a visa at the UK Embassy. Upon receiving the documents, Zvina went to the UK Embassy to apply for the visas for himself, Fari, and Jeni. But before he handed in his application, he had to find out how long it would take to get the visas. Jill had said that she wanted them to join her within two weeks, since she was lonely. If the processing time for the visas would be longer than two weeks, she would rather they just leave Zimbabwe without the visas. They would just get visitors' visas at the port of entry and then apply for the long stay visas after they arrived in the UK. At that time, Zimbabweans were not required to get a visitor's visa prior to their departure to the UK. They could get them at the port of entry. When Zvina was told that the processing time for their visa application would be more than six weeks, he decided not to submit the application. Instead, as suggested by Jill, they would depart without visas and get visitors' visas when they arrived in the UK.

When Zvina left the Embassy, he went straight to his travel agent to book the flights. He decided to leave in a week. There was nothing to wait for. However, he wondered if his departure to the UK would affect his work permit application in Canada. He pondered over this for a while and decided to stop by a pub. He needed more time to think before booking the flights. He ordered a beer and sat down in a quiet dark corner. As he sat in that dark corner, he constantly scratched his head and pulled his hair. He was clearly agitated.

"Is everything ok, Sir?" asked the waitress. She set a bottle of beer and a chilled glass on the table in front of Zvina.

"Oh yes," replied Zvina, "I'm just tired."

"Shall I pour the beer in the glass for you?"

"No worries. Thanks. I can do it."

"Ok. I will check on you in a while. If you finish the beer before I come, just call me."

"Ok. Thanks."

As Zvina drank his beer, a whirlwind of thoughts raced through his mind. He wondered what would happen with the Canadian work permit application if he left for the UK. Was he supposed to tell them that he was moving to the

UK or not? If he moved, then the Embassy would require his new contact information. However, if he gave them his new contact information, would that slow down the work permit application process since they would have to update his file? Would they require more information as to why he was moving to the UK, despite the fact that he had applied for a work permit in Canada? Would they think that he was not serious about his work permit application? If he did not inform them about his move to the UK, they might require him to go to South Africa for a permit application interview. Could he afford to fly back to Africa for a permit application interview? He did not yet have any savings in the UK. Since they would require him to send his passport once the permit was approved, what would they do if they saw the UK visa in his passport? Would they say he had lied to them about living in Zimbabwe?

After drinking a couple of beers and pondering over these questions that were racing through his mind, Zvina concluded that he had to proceed with the plan to go to the UK. He would write a letter to the Canadian Embassy and inform them of his move. He would explain why he had to move and provide his new contact information. He would also emphasize his desire to move to Canada if his work permit application was successful. He thought this was the right move, since he had no idea when his permit application would be approved. He could not continue to stay in Zimbabwe indefinitely. It was also time he went back to work. Due to the worsening economic situation in Zimbabwe, there were no jobs. In the UK, he could find a job, even a temporary one. If push came to shove and the work permit for Canada did not come, and if he could not find suitable work in the UK, then he was prepared to go back to school to do a Master's degree. Having made up his mind, he finished up his beer, paid his bill, and left the pub. He would go to his travel agent, Sarah, and book the earliest flight available for Fari, Jeni, and himself. He was lucky to get booked on a flight that was only six days away.

After booking the flight, Zvina started making arrangements for his departure. First and most important, he wrote a letter to the Canadian Embassy to inform them of his move to the UK and to give them his new contact information. Since he knew his case officer's name, he decided to also call her and give her the information. This way, he would be one hundred percent certain that she had his new contact information.

The following morning, he wrote the letter and posted it. When he got back home from the post office, he called his case officer. Fortunately, he got through without any issues. He quickly gave his case officer his new contact information. Before hanging up he asked her how long she thought it would take for the permit to come out. As usual, the answer was that she did not know.

"That's done and out of the way," he said after hanging up. "I will be leaving in five days. What am I supposed to do before I leave? I have to visit the same people and places that we visited with Jill before she left. I should be able to do all of this in the next three or four days. I don't want to be running around on the last day."

The next four days were very busy for Zvina. His first trip out of town was to Madziva to see Jill's grandmother. This time around it was just him, Fari, and Jeni. They spent the night in Madziva and left for Bindura around noon the next day. In Bindura, they passed through Jill's uncle's farm before proceeding to spend the night at his sister's place. The next day, they left Bindura early in the afternoon on their way back to Harare. They visited Zvina's uncle in Kuwadzana and spent the night there. Their next trip was to Bocha to see Zvina's father. They left Harare early in the morning. This time around they picked up Simo and Tangai, Zvina's brother.

They arrived in Mutare just before midday. Everybody was hungry, so they stopped at Nando's and had lunch. After lunch, they went to TM hyper supermarket and bought some groceries.

They arrived in Bocha just before sunset. There was no one at home. This time of the year, people in rural areas were usually outside preparing their fields before the rainy season.

"I think Sekuru and Mama (Zvina's stepmother) have gone to the fields," said Zvina as he tried to open the main door to the house.

"Do you want to follow them to the fields, or should we send the herdboy to tell them we are here?" asked Tangai.

"No. Let them carry on with their work. It won't be long before the sun sets. They will be here soon," replied Zvina, sitting down on the veranda.

"What time are we leaving tomorrow?" asked Simo, as he came to sit down next to Zvina.

"Early afternoon. We have to be in Harare before sunset," replied Zvina.

"Ok. In that case, don't you want to have one or two at the liquor store at Mafararikwa Primary School, so you can bid your old folks farewell?"

"Good idea, Simo. Let's leave right away. We have to get back soon. I want to spend as much time with my father as possible."

Zvina and Simo got into the car and left for Mafararikwa Primary School. When they got there most of the stores were relatively quiet except Dururu's liquor store. A big speaker on the veranda was playing music at maximum volume. There were about twenty men at Dururu's liquor store. Some of them were playing a game called draft on the store's veranda. Draft is a board game played on a board similar to a chess board. The rules are different though, and bottle caps are used instead of chess pieces. Some younger men were dancing to the music while others stood or sat in little groups chatting away over beer. There were very few of them drinking clear beer. Most of them were drinking opaque beer from the same big mug, which they passed around. When Zvina pulled up in front of the bottle store, everybody stopped what they were doing to look at him. A few of them called out, "Mawira! Mawira!"

Some of the men came over to the car to greet Zvina. Zvina and Simo got out of the car and greeted everybody before joining a group that was sitting on the veranda. After exchanging greetings in the traditional way, Zvina bought a round of beer for everyone in the group. After another round of beers, Zvina and Simo left just after sunset.

When they got back home, everybody was already home. Sekuru was sitting on his reclining garden chair under the tree in front of the house. Tangai and others were sitting around Sekuru. All of the women were inside the kitchen preparing supper. Zvina got out of the car, hugged Sekuru, and started crying. This surprised Sekuru.

"What is it, my son?" he asked. Zvina did not answer him. He kept crying.

"Simo! What has happened to him?" Sekuru turned around to ask Simo.

"Nothing has happened to him. He has been fine all this time," replied Simo.

"I think I know what it is. He is just overcome with emotions. He is going to miss you, Baba, when he is gone," Tangai chimed in.

"Ok. It's going to be alright, my son," said Sekuru, patting Zvina on the back.

A moment of silence followed as Zvina cried while Sekuru continuously patted him on the back. When Zvina stopped crying, he wiped the tears off his cheeks and sat down on the ground next to Sekuru.

Another minute of silence followed. Everybody looked down on the ground and remained still. Simo finally broke the silence: "Zvina! Tell Sekuru your troubles. He is the only medium through which your troubles can be brought before the ancestors and God Almighty."

"Thanks, Simo," said Zvina. He quivered a little bit before continuing, "Baba! I don't know what's happening in my life. I don't know why I am so unlucky. I want to go to Canada, but the permit application is taking forever to come out. Who knows? It may never come out. What is it, Baba?" He started crying again.

"Well, it's..."

"But Baba!" Zvina interjected, "it's been over eight months now and there is no indication that the permit will come out soon. For others, these applications take less than six months.

Why is it taking so long for me? Did I do anything wrong to deserve this? I just want to go and work in Canada."

"I hear you, my son."

"I don't want to go to the UK. Now I have no choice but to go there. I was hoping that by now I would have the permit and I wouldn't have to go to the UK. I don't deserve this."

"Mukanya! It's going to be alright. Everything has a reason. Someday the reason will be revealed to you. This delay might make you thank God and the ancestors because something unpleasant will have been prevented from happening in your life. Anyway, I will let Mupare (Zvina's late great-grandmother) and Mawira (Zvina's late great-grandfather) know your situation. These two will bring this before the Almighty. I have faith that they will remove all the obstacles in your way so that you can achieve what you desire. This will be the main subject of our prayer tonight," said Sekuru, in a very reassuring, firm voice.

Zvina stood up and went into the kitchen to greet the women. Mama was as loud as usual, telling the girls what to do around the stove. Fari was on Mama's back. Mama always liked carrying babies on her back. When Fari saw Zvina coming in, he started fidgeting around so he could come down. Mama let him down and Fari ran to sit on his dad's lap.

After supper, everyone went into the kitchen. They talked about many things for hours.

"It's time we went to bed," said Sekuru as he broke into a chorus. Everybody joined in and they sang for a few minutes.

"Let's pray."

Everybody went on their knees and Sekuru began to pray.

"Mwaisapai, my mother! Mupare, my grandmother! Muchadrya, my great-uncle; and Kuvengawafa, my

great-granduncle; and you, Mawira, the great soldier; you are all sitting next to the throne of the Almighty. I come before you tonight with peace and hope. I thank you for bringing my son Zvina before the Almighty. My son is crying before you, my Lord. I plead with you to take control of his life. You are the Almighty, the lord of Israel. May Zvina's wishes be fulfilled. There are so many obstacles and enemies on this Earth, but nothing is impossible with you, my Lord. May your will be done in Zvina's life. When he leaves this country to go overseas to find that treasure he is looking for, I pray that your light shines down upon all of his pathways. Help him open all the doors he wants to open. Lead him and bless him on his way out, and on his way back in. Let him sing Hosanna! Hosanna! at sunrise and sunset. I also bring before you his wife and son. You are the light in their lives. I pray for endless love between Zvina and his wife. Make them look after and look out for each other. I pray for those of us that they are leaving behind. Please make us think of them and pray for them every day. Let their nostalgia be prayers to you, so you can bring them back to us while our bodies and souls are still together. I call upon you again, Mwaisapai, my mother. Mupare, my grandmother. Muchadrya, my great-uncle; and Kuvengawafa, my great-granduncle; and you, Mawira, the great soldier; that is my request to you tonight. Pass it on to the Almighty. I thank you. Let us all say the daily prayer."

Everybody joined in the daily prayer.

"Our Father, who art in heaven…"

After the prayer, everyone went to bed.

The next morning, Zvina, Tangai, and Simo joined Sekuru in the field. After they had tilled about half a ridge, Sekuru excused himself and went back home. He had a few things to do at home in preparation for Zvina's departure. Zvina and the others continued tilling until late morning. When they got home, the herdboy was skinning a goat and Fari sat close by, quietly watching.

"Zvina," shouted Mama, laughing at the same time, "look at your son. He is a true meat lover. Everybody thought he would be scared seeing a goat being skinned, but he isn't. He even touched it before they killed it. I don't know where he gets this fearlessness from. Maybe from his big daddy Timbo."

"I think so too," said Zvina, walking towards Fari. "Fari! Are you not afraid?"

Fari turned around to look at his dad. He smiled, pointing at the carcass.

"That's meat. Do you know that?" said Zvina, picking Fari up and walking away from the scene.

"No! Dad no! Put me down!" Fari screamed as his dad tried to take him away.

"You want to watch this?"

"Yes," replied Fari, nodding.

"Ok." Zvina put him down and left.

Sekuru had ordered that a goat be slaughtered. He wanted the family to have a big farewell lunch for Zvina. He had even invited a few of his close cousins and friends. After lunch, Sekuru called Zvina into the house. It would be a private talk, so he closed and locked the door.

"My son," he began, "I have heard what you said about things not working out according to your plans. All of this is in the hands of the ancestors and God now. Expect change going forward. You will be successful in your plans. Do not be afraid of anything. Do not worry about anything. The ancestors and God are with you all the time, and they will lead your way. I will be with you in spirit all the time."

Sekuru went into his bedroom and brought a small used bottle. He opened the bottle and took a sip of the liquid that was inside.

"There is water in this bottle. I have anointed it. Here, drink it," he passed the bottle to Zvina.

Zvina took a sip and handed the bottle back to Sekuru.

"Good. I want you to take this bottle with you. Keep it with you wherever you go. I don't mean on you all the time, but in your house where you live. Drink it from time to time. It will cleanse you and protect you from all kinds of evil. Do not let it run out. When it gets low, top it up before it is empty. This way it will remain anointed."

Sekuru handed the bottle back to Zvina.

"Ok, Baba. I will do that," Zvina promised.

"Safe travels, and don't forget us. When you get settled, I want you to come home every year. It doesn't have to be at Christmas time. Any time of the year is good. The most important thing is that we get to see each other from time to time. Our days on this Earth are numbered. We have to spend as much time together as possible. Don't worry about us here. We have the fields to till and harvest, and we get some cash from the rental house in Bulawayo. We can survive. As I said, all we need is to see you here every year. That's it. Fambai zvakanaka Mukanya *(Safe travels Mukanya)*. Let's join everybody outside. You must get ready to leave so you don't have to drive after sunset."

Zvina and Sekuru joined the men sitting under the mulberry tree. Soon it was time for Zvina and his team to leave.

They packed up their belongings in the car, bade farewell to everyone, and left for Harare.

When he got back to Harare, Zvina spent the last three days before his departure visiting close relatives and friends around Harare. He closed all of his bank and utility accounts. As per tradition, on his departure day, friends and relatives drove him, Fari, and Jeni to the airport.

Chapter Eight

Arrival in The United Kingdom

"Hello, Sir. Welcome to the UK. May I have your passport, please?" said an immigration officer.

Zvina handed the immigration officer three passports: his, his son's, and his sister-in-law's.

"Are you all in the same family?"

"Yes," replied Zvina.

The officer took the passports and placed them on the counter before asking, "Where are you arriving from?"

"Zimbabwe," replied Zvina.

"Are you citizens of Zimbabwe?"

"Yes," replied Zvina.

The officer picked up one passport and started carefully perusing through the pages.

"No visa in this one. I guess this is the first time the kid has left Zimbabwe," said the officer, putting the passport down on the counter and picking up another one. Once again, he carefully perused through the passport. It took him about five minutes to go through all of the pages in the passport before he lifted his head and asked, "I see you have travelled quite a bit. You were here in the UK a couple of times earlier in the year. What brings you back to the UK again?"

"My wife got a job with Lloyds Pharmacies here in the UK. She is now working here. I have come to join her," replied Zvina.

"Oh! Is that right? Good for her. So obviously this is your son?"

"Yes."

"And is she your daughter?" asked the officer, pointing to Jeni.

"No. She is my sister-in-law," replied Zvina.

"Ok. We will come back to her later. Let's process you and your son first," said the officer. He picked up Zvina's passport and began going through it again.

"So how long are you two going to stay in UK with your wife?" asked the officer.

This question baffled Zvina. He frowned for a second before replying, "My wife got a three-year work permit. We have come to stay with her while she works here. So, you could say three years."

"I don't see your visa anywhere in the passport."

"No, we don't have visas. We were told that we can get the visas at the port of entry."

"Who told you that?"

"An officer at the British High Commission in Harare."

"They either lied to you, or they did not understand your question. You can only get a visitor's visa at the port of entry. For a long stay visa like what you want to get, you have to apply at the British Embassy in your country of origin and you must have it in your possession before you leave for the UK. We may have to send you back to Zimbabwe," said the officer, as he placed Zvina's passport down. He picked up Jeni's passport and quickly scanned through it.

"No visa in this one either. So why are you visiting the UK, and where are you going in the UK?" the officer asked Jeni. Before Jeni could reply, Zvina quickly jumped in,

"Like I said before, she is my sister-in-law. She is coming to stay with us."

"Why is she coming to stay with you? How long will she stay with you before she goes back to Zimbabwe?" asked the officer.

"She will probably stay for a month or two. It will depend on how fast we get settled here in the UK. Since we don't have any relatives where we will be staying, we thought we could use her company."

"Where are you going to be staying in the UK?"

"Sheffield, West Yorkshire."

"Ok. Does your sister-in-law work or go to school in Zimbabwe?"

"No."

"So why would she have any reason to go back to Zimbabwe?"

"Because that's her home country. I thought you would give her a visitor's visa for that duration and when it expires she would go back to Zimbabwe."

"Not many people do that, Sir. They stay in the UK illegally." The officer paused, and then continued, "Anyway, I don't want to waste everyone's time here. I think we have to send you all back to Zimbabwe on the next available flight. Please take all of your belongings and come with me."

This was a big blow in the face for Zvina. It reminded him of what had happened to him in Canada. He did not want to go through the same experience again, especially not with his two-and-a-half-year-old son. They obediently picked up their luggage and followed the officer to a room packed with travellers, mostly Africans and Asians.

"Find somewhere to sit in here. I will come back to see you later," said the officer before walking away with all of their passports.

As they waited for the officer to tell them their fate, Zvina thought about all of the possibilities, including the worst-case scenario and what he wished for. The worst-case scenario for him would be spending several days or months in detention. This was definitely not desirable. He did not want to spend any time in a detention centre with his son. He wondered if they had detention camps for families. He had never heard of family detention centres. If they did not have family detention centres, would they separate him from his son and detain him in a children's detention centre? Would they have children's detention centres? That would be illegal. What would happen? He wondered. Zvina just sat there and hoped for a miracle that they would let them into the UK. However, if they did not let them in, he would rather be on a flight back to Zimbabwe that night. Although this was his second favourite possibility, it was still hard to swallow. He missed his wife and he knew his son did too. They could not wait to reunite with Jill. Going back to Zimbabwe would mean at least another two months before him and Fari could reunite with his wife. It would be painful to be apart for so long. While he was lost in thought, Zvina fell into a deep sleep. He had started making some noises by the time his sister-in-law shook him awake. When he woke up he almost jumped off the bench that he was sitting on. He looked around and saw that almost everyone in the room was looking at him. He was very embarrassed.

"You must be very tired, Sir," an old man sitting on the other side of the room said kindly. "Long flight, hey?"

"Yes," replied Zvina.

After about an hour the officer came back and asked Zvina to follow him into a small room that was nearby. Zvina picked up his son and asked his sister-in-law to come with them.

"She does not have to come. I just need you alone. You can bring the kid with you, if you like," said the officer.

Jeni went back to her seat.

When they got into the room, the officer showed Zvina a chair and asked him to sit down.

"Before we can decide on what to do with you, Sir, I would like to get some more information," began the officer.

"Ok," replied Zvina.

"You said that your wife got a work permit and she is now working here in the UK. Do you have her work permit, or a copy of it with you?" asked the officer.

"Yes, I do."

"May I have it please?"

Zvina pulled out a copy of Jill's work permit from his bag and handed it over to the officer. The officer took the copy and left the room. After about half an hour, he came back and handed the permit back to Zvina.

"Where does your wife live in the UK?"

"Sheffield."

"Does she have a contact number I can reach her at?"

"She does not have a personal phone. I can give you her work phone number but she is not at work today."

"Where is she?"

"She is on her way to meet us here."

"Ok. Does she own a house in Sheffield?"

"No. She doesn't. She is renting."

"How big is the place she is renting?"

"It's a two–bedroom terrace."

"Do you know how much she is paying for rent?"

"No, I don't."

"Do you know how much she makes per month?"

"She told me but I can't remember."

"Do you intend to look for work in the UK?"

"Yes, I do."

"What type of work?"

"I am an engineer."

"Which engineering?"

"Metallurgical engineering."

"What's that?"

"Mineral processing."

"Oh! So, you work in the mines?"

"Yes."

"Which company did you work for in Zimbabwe?"

"I worked for Anglo American Corporation."

"Ok. How long did you work for Anglo American?"

"Five years."

"Is your wife going to renew her work permit when it expires in three years?"

"I don't know."

The officer picked up Zvina's passport and started perusing through the pages again. After a while, he looked up and asked, "Have you ever been denied entry into any country?"

"No."

"Have you ever been deported from any country for any reason?"

"No."

"Have you ever over-stayed in any country before?"

"No."

"You have been in Canada and the UK a couple of times within a short period of time. What was the reason for your travels?"

"I visited my uncle in Canada and on my way back I passed through the UK to visit my mum and auntie. While I was in the UK I was contacted by a Canadian company that wanted to interview me for a job there. I returned to Canada to attend the interview."

"What happened with that job?"

"I got the job but I am not eligible to work in Canada. I applied for a work permit. It is still being processed."

"So why do you want a visa to stay in the UK if you are going to end up going to Canada?"

"Well, when my wife got the opportunity to come and work in the UK, we were not sure if I would get the permit for Canada. Even now, I am not sure. Anything can happen, you know. We can't let other opportunities go by while we wait for that."

"If your work permit does come out, will you stay in the UK, or will you move to Canada?"

"Well, it depends on what is happening in our lives at the time it comes out."

"What do you mean?"

"I mean, if it comes out after I have settled in the UK and gotten myself a good job, better than the job in Canada, I may not move. I will have to evaluate the two options based on a number of factors, I guess."

"Have you already applied for jobs in the UK?"

"No, I haven't."

"Ok, Sir. I will be back in a few minutes."

The officer stood up and left the room. In the meantime, Zvina was left wondering. The officer had asked him many questions, some of which he thought were not relevant. He wondered if this was a sign that they would be letting him into the UK. If they were not going to let him into the UK, there was no reason for the officer to waste so much time asking Zvina all of these questions.

They had been at the airport for more than two hours now. Zvina knew that his wife and brother were waiting for them in the Arrivals Hall. By now, they would be anxiously wondering what was delaying Zvina inside the airport. He wished he had a way of contacting them. His son, who was obviously very tired, was starting to get irritated. Zvina picked him up from the floor where he was lying and put him on his lap.

"Are you tired?" he asked his son.

"Yes. I want Mummy. You said Mummy will be here. Where is she?"

"She is waiting for us outside."

"Let's go. What are we doing here? I want Mummy."

"We will be out soon. We just want the officer to give us our passports back and we will be on our way out."

"Where is he?"

"He has gone to another office. He will be back shortly."

The officer walked in and sat down. He placed the passports on the table and opened a file that he had brought with him. He flipped through the papers in the file for some time. After a while he looked up and said, "Ok. You are good to go. Welcome to the United Kingdom. Enjoy your stay."

He handed two passports back to Zvina.

Zvina took the passports and checked them. This was a big relief for Zvina, but his relief was very short-lived when he realized that the officer had not given him his sister-in-law's passport.

"What about Jeni's passport? I see you did not give it to me," Zvina said.

"No, I haven't. Jeni is an adult. She has to be interviewed on her own."

"I know, but I am travelling with her and I am responsible for her."

"That's your arrangement with her, not us. As far as we are concerned, she is an adult and therefore she has to be interviewed by herself."

"She does not have the necessary information that you will be wanting from her."

"You can give me all of the information or documentation that we require. If we need more information, we can ask you or contact your wife," said the officer. He got up and walked towards the door. "Please come with me to the waiting room," the officer said.

When they got to the waiting room, they saw that Jeni had fallen asleep while waiting. Zvina woke her up and the officer who still had Jeni's passport in his hand asked her to follow him.

"Ma'am, please come with me."

Zvina quickly stepped up and said to Jeni in Shona, "Whatever questions they ask you, just tell them that you are accompanying us and will stay with us for a month. You will be going back to college in Zimbabwe, so you must go back. Tell them we sponsored you and you have no money because you do not work back in Zimbabwe. Ok? Do not change your statement. Stick to it or they will send you back home. If you are not sure about an answer, tell them you don't know. Good luck."

"Has he given you your visas already?" asked Jeni in Shona.

"Yes, he gave visas to me and Fari. Go ahead and follow him. He is waiting for you. You don't want to make him impatient or angry with you."

Jeni followed the officer and they disappeared down the hallway.

About an hour later the officer came back with Jeni following behind him. He had Jeni's documents in his hand and Jeni was crying. This was not a good sign. That meant they had not given Jeni the entry visa. They were going to send her back to Zimbabwe. This devastated Zvina. As soon as Fari saw that Jeni was crying, he jumped off of Zvina's lap and ran towards her. As Fari hugged Jeni by her waist, Jeni could not contain herself. She cried even more.

"Sir, I am sorry we cannot let your sister-in-law into the UK. We have no reasonable grounds to believe that she will go back to Zimbabwe," said the officer.

"But…" Zvina tried to speak, but he was choking with anger and frustration.

"There is nothing I can do for you. It's the law. We are going to send her back to Zimbabwe on the next available flight."

Zvina was dumbfounded. Jeni continued to sob even louder at this point. Fari was clamouring at Jeni for attention, but Jeni paid no attention to him. She was sobbing so loudly that everybody in the waiting room was now looking at her. For a few moments, everybody in the waiting room seemed to be commiserating with Jeni. They were all waiting to undergo the same process. Their fate was unknown at this time. Only heaven knew, and only time had the answer. The officer must have felt bad to be in the midst of such miserable people. He was quick to announce his intention to leave.

"Ok. Ma'am, we have to leave. Get all your stuff and follow me."

Zvina walked over to Jeni and Fari, hugged them both, and said to Jeni, "Don't worry. Just do what they say. If you have to go back to Zimbabwe, that's fine. We will send money to apply for a visa from there and you will come and join us. We, especially Fari, are going to miss you, but we will make sure you visit us in the next few months."

Jeni was too overwhelmed to say anything. She just nodded and lifted Fari up before kissing him and handing him over to Zvina. They picked up their luggage and followed the officer back to the front counter.

"Sir, you and the kid can go. I will arrange to have your sister-in-law taken to detention."

Zvina, Jeni, and Fari hugged before Zvina and Fari left for the Arrivals Hall.

At the Arrivals Hall, Jill and Zvina's brother, Timbo, were waiting for them. Fari was surprised to see his mum.

"Wow! Mum!" Fari shouted as he ran towards his mum.

"You guys took a long time to come out. We were worried. It's been three hours since you landed. Where is Jeni?" asked Jill as she picked up Fari.

"It's a long story," said Zvina as he greeted his brother. "I was getting worried that you guys might have thought that we had been denied entry and gone back home."

"We were here. We would not go anywhere until we could confirm what had happened to you. Where is my sister?" asked Jill anxiously.

"They would not let her in," replied Zvina.

"Why?"

"They grilled us big time. I will tell you what happened on the way home. They said they would not let Jeni in because they had no reasonable grounds to believe that she would be going back to Zimbabwe. They would not even interview her in my presence, so I couldn't help her."

"What are they going to do with her?"

"Guys, let's go to the car and get out of here. It's getting late. We have a long way to drive," said Timbo.

Timbo had placed all of their luggage on a trolley, and he led the way to the parkade.

"You did not tell me what they are going to do with my sister," Jill repeated.

"They said that they would be sending her back home on the next available flight. But for now, they are sending her to a detention camp," replied Zvina.

"Well. As long as they send her back home and do not keep her in detention for a long time, I am ok with that. She must be devastated."

"Oh! She is. She was crying from the time she came back from the interview room until we left."

"We will have to send her money to apply for a visitor's visa soon," said Jill.

When they got to the car, they loaded up their luggage and left Gatwick International Airport. Timbo drove them to Sheffield.

In Sheffield, Jill had a two-bedroom terrace house rented in the neighbourhood of Hillsborough. It was not the best of neighbourhoods, but she had chosen it because it was convenient for her commute to work. It was also affordable.

For his first few weeks in the UK, Zvina babysat Fari while Jill went to work. Zvina spent most his time on the internet looking for jobs. At first, he was specifically looking for an engineering job at a mine, smelter, refinery, or foundry. He had his eyes on Sheffield Steel Works. At one time, he landed an interview with a small family-run foundry, but he never heard back from them after the interview. Soon he realized that the type of engineering jobs he was looking for were very difficult to find in the UK. He was getting sick and tired of babysitting. One day he started discussing some alternatives with his wife.

"Honey, I am getting sick and tired of this job search. I don't seem to see many openings that are suitable for me. I have not received any replies from the few suitable openings that I have applied for. I need to start working," said Zvina to his wife.

"I was hoping you would find something suitable in the steel industry here. I am surprised it's proving to be difficult."

"Yes, me too. I wish they would approve my visa application in Canada. I would not waste time here."

"You are right. It's so frustrating that you have a job in a country where you are not allowed to work, but you can't find a job in a country where you are allowed to live and work."

"I don't know why the Canadians take so long to process a work permit application. In Zimbabwe, the doctor said that my high blood pressure should not be of concern. The results are acceptable. I wonder what is delaying my work permit."

"Maybe we just have to be patient."

"But I need to be doing something now."

"Honey, I know what you mean. We will be fine; just be patient. Give them another month or so, and if nothing happens, we can start looking seriously at other options."

There was silence in the room. Fari was lying on his tummy watching TV. He was watching his favourite show and paying no attention to his parents' discussion.

"Did you give the Canadian Embassy our UK contact number in case they want to contact you?" asked Jill.

"Yes, I did. They have my email address too," Zvina said.

"I have a feeling it's getting close. Let's just keep our fingers crossed," Jill said hopefully.

"Did you call UK Immigration to find out about Jeni?" asked Zvina.

"Yes, I did. They were going to send her back home a few days ago," Jill answered. She got up to turn the lights on.

"What happened?" Zvina asked again.

"She has claimed asylum. So, they could not send her back," replied Jill.

"Is that right?"

"Yes. Once you claim asylum, they cannot deport you until your case is brought to the court of law before a judge. The judge makes the final ruling after hearing your case." Jill sounded as though she was very knowledgeable on the subject.

"Really? I wasn't aware of that. Did they tell you how long this process takes? Going to court is usually a long process.

It could take several months, if not years. I would rather go back home than stay in a detention camp for several months," said Zvina, with a hint of disapproval in his voice.

"They said that they don't keep people in detention camps while they are waiting for their cases to go to court. They rent them houses and give them a living allowance until the judge has made a ruling on their cases," Jill explained, clearly defending her sister's decision to seek political asylum.

"Where are these rental houses? In London?" Zvina asked again, rather sarcastically.

"They said that these rental houses are located all over the UK. They did not tell me where they will be sending Jeni, because they haven't determined that yet. But I will call them next week. They will know by then." Jill paused for a moment, and then continued, "I hope they send her to a city close to Sheffield, so we can visit her and she can visit us from time to time."

"For sure. Fari would be happy," said Zvina.

As Zvina and Jill settled into their new lives in the UK, they had to adjust to a few things. In Zimbabwe, they had been used to having lots of friends and relatives around them. This was not the case in Sheffield. They did not know anyone there. In Zimbabwe, there was always something happening on weekends. It could be anything from a party or barbeque at a friend's or relative's house to a trip to the rural areas. But nothing like that ever happened in Sheffield. They spent most of their weekends watching movies at home.

They also missed their staple foods, especially sadza (cornmeal). They had gone to all of the grocery stores around town, including the ethnic stores, but they could not find cornmeal or any other foods that were close to their staple foods. They had been told that the only place to find the ethnic foods they wanted was London. So, they were planning to stock up on supplies the next time they went to London.

The couple had introduced themselves to their neighbours and had started to try and build some relationships with them. To their surprise, the neighbours did not seem too keen on making friends with them. Instead, the neighbours preferred to mind their own business.

Regardless of these issues, Jill and Zvina were happy to be in the UK. The UK had the economic and political stability that they were looking for. At one time they had contemplated moving to London where Zvina's mum and siblings were. They also had several cousins that lived in London. Certainly, life would have been a lot better in London than Sheffield. After careful consideration, they decided to stay in Sheffield. They knew that things would get better in the future. Jill would start by making friends at work, and they would take it from there. They were also going to try and find out if there were other Zimbabweans living in Sheffield or other nearby cities.

Five weeks after their arrival, Zvina started looking for any kind of job he could get. He just wanted to get out of the house and work. He was prepared to do anything that would keep him active mentally as well as physically. This meant that they would have to send Fari to daycare. But at that point, they could not afford daycare. They decided to take Fari to London to stay with his grandmother.

Chapter Nine

The Big Blow! Was it Coincidence?

One morning, while Zvina was in the library browsing the journals and periodicals for jobs, he received a call from the Canadian Embassy in South Africa. They told him that his work permit had been approved. They wanted him to send his family's passports, so that they could issue the visas. Zvina was ecstatic. He quickly called Jill and told her the good news. He rushed back home to get the passports and sent them to South Africa by DHL. When he got back home, Jill was home from work and preparing dinner.

"Hi sweetie!" said Zvina, kissing Jill on the cheek.

"Hi. How are you?"

"Couldn't be better! The permit is now approved. Canada, here we come!" exclaimed Zvina, opening the fridge to get a bottle of beer.

"I am relieved. This has been a painful journey. I am glad we are finally there. Thank God. Did you send the passports?"

"Yes. They will be at the Canadian Embassy in South Africa tomorrow afternoon. I will arrange to have them picked up by DHL once the visas are issued."

"I hope that will not take weeks," Jill said worriedly.

"I asked them when they called me, and they said it could take up to two weeks," Zvina informed her.

"I don't understand how these people work. How can it take two weeks to just stamp visas in three passports? Only heaven knows," Jill mused.

"It's a process. The passports and visas probably have to be reviewed by a number of people before they are finalized. I am just happy that the permit has been approved. Two weeks is nothing. We have come a long way since I first submitted the application," Zvina noted.

"I wonder how much longer the permanent residency application is going take. Did you send them a letter notifying them of our change of address?" asked Jill.

"Yes, I did," confirmed Zvina.

"How long has it been since you submitted the application?" Jill asked.

"Over eighteen months," replied Zvina. "I also sent them my job offer from Cominco. They say it helps in their decision process if the applicant has a job in Canada already."

"I guess it doesn't really matter now. We will be living in Canada anyway. How long is the work permit valid for?" asked Jill.

"Three years," answered Zvina.

"The residency permit should be out in less than three years. Can you renew the work permit?" asked Jill again.

"Yes, I can. I hope we won't have to. We will be permanent residents by the time the permit expires," said Zvina hopefully.

"So, you need to contact Cominco to let them know that the permit has been approved," Jill suggested.

"Sure. I will do that. I think the lawyer will also inform them. Once we get the passports back, Cominco will need to know so that they can start making arrangements for me to start work."

"Are they going to pay for the flights and everything when we go to Canada?" asked Jill.

"I am not sure. I will find out."

"We also need to decide if we are going to go at the same time, or if you will go first and then me and Fari will follow once you are settled."

"I will have to find out about that as well. I am guessing that they will pay for our flights and accommodation for a given time while we look for our own accommodation," Zvina speculated.

"Have you told anyone that you got the work permit?" asked Jill.

"No. Anything can happen between now and the day we get the passports back. I will only tell people when I see the visas stamped in our passports."

"You are right. Let's wait until we get the passports back," said Jill as she dished food onto plates on the countertop next to the stove.

"I know it's a done deal and we should be celebrating, but I don't want to tell anyone until we get the passports back," Zvina repeated.

"Dinner is ready. Do you want to sit at the dining table or in the living room?"

"Let's sit in the living room so we can watch TV while we eat," said Zvina as he walked towards Jill to get his food.

"Ok. Here you are," said Jill, passing Zvina a plate of food.

They went into the living room and ate their dinner while watching TV.

"Thanks for the dinner. I will wash the dishes," said Zvina, taking Jill's empty plate. After washing the dishes, he rejoined Jill in the living room.

"I think I will send Cominco an email to let them know that the permit has been approved," said Zvina. He got up to go to their bedroom where their workstation was.

"Good idea," affirmed Jill.

When Zvina opened his email, he was surprised to see that he had an email from the Human Resources manager at Cominco. In his mind, he quickly concluded that the Human Resources manager had contacted him to start processing his move.

"Honey! The HR manager sent me an email already. I think they want me to start ASAP," Zvina shouted to his wife.

"What are they saying?" Jill shouted back.

"I am just opening the email. I haven't read it yet," replied Zvina.

When he opened the email, Zvina could not believe it. The Human Resources Manager had written to let him know that Cominco was withdrawing its offer of employment to him because the permit had taken too long to come out.

He stood up in front of the computer desk, looked up in the air, and sighed. He sat down at the computer desk again and read the email for the second time, very slowly this time.

"Hey honey! What are they saying in the email?" asked Jill from the living room.

"You won't believe this," replied Zvina.

"What?"

"They are withdrawing the job offer."

"You are kidding me! Did they say why?"

"Yes. They said that it is taking too long for the permit to come out," said Zvina with a tremble in his voice.

"Well, it's out now," shouted Jill from the living room.

"But they have withdrawn the offer," said Zvina, going down the stairs to the living room.

"That should not be a problem. They wrote the email today. You have been told that the permit has been approved today. If you reply to their email and tell them that the permit has been approved, then they will reverse their decision. I don't think they would have hired someone to fill that position already. If anything, they would have started advertising today to fill the position" said Jill confidently.

"Usually big organizations like this don't reverse their decisions easily," said Zvina rather pessimistically.

"This is a rather unique situation. They are hiring you from overseas, which means they really like you. They have spent money hiring an immigration lawyer to help process your permit. They cannot just let that money go for nothing. I don't think their lawyer has informed them that the permit has been approved. The Canadian Embassy probably didn't tell the lawyer yet."

Zvina kept pacing back and forth in the living room. He could not sit down.

"I don't think you should worry. Go back upstairs and reply to their email. Tell them the permit has been approved," Jill tried to reassure her husband.

"I can't. This is devastating. My mind is not clear now. I can't even type. My hands are shaking."

"Oh sweetie! Come on," said Jill, getting up and hugging Zvina. "Don't worry. Let's go back upstairs and I will type the email for you."

"Maybe I just need to calm down and reply to the email tomorrow."

"No. You will be wasting time, and if they want to hire someone else for that position, they might start the process right away. Let's reply to that email now," Jill insisted.

She grabbed Zvina by his hand and they went upstairs to the computer desk.

"The email is still open. I didn't close it."

"Ok. Let me type for you. I will make it a very short reply. You don't want to make it too long, otherwise they won't read it."

Jill sat down at the computer desk and replied to the email. It was a very short email that was straight to the point.

Dear Human Resources Manager,

Thank you very much for the email I just received. What a coincidence. I also received a call from the Canadian Embassy in South Africa today and they told me that the work permit has been approved. They asked me to send them my passport and I sent it immediately after the call. I hope this is timely enough for Cominco to reverse its decision to withdraw the job offer.

Thank you.
Sincerely,
Zvina Mawira

While Jill wrote the email, Zvina paced back and forth.

"I am done. Come and read it before I send it," said Jill, getting off the chair.

"You can sit. I will read it while standing. It's ok," said Zvina, leaning over the desk.

He read the email a couple of times before asking Jill to send it.

"I think this is all you need to do. Let's go and watch TV. You will definitely hear from them by tomorrow evening at the latest, and I can guarantee you they will reverse their decision."

"I would like to agree with you, but at the back of my mind something tells me that this opportunity has slipped out of my hands. Anyway, let's wait and see."

"You have to be positive, my dear," said Jill shutting down the computer.

They went downstairs and watched TV before going to bed.

Zvina lay awake for hours that night. He couldn't stop thinking about the email from Cominco. A few times he thought he was having a bad dream. After pinching himself or shaking his wife, he would realize that he was not dreaming. First thing the next morning, he checked his email. Unfortunately, he had not received any new emails from Cominco. He had hoped that they would have replied to his email before the end of the previous day. They hadn't. This was going to make the day a very long one for him since he would now have to wait until evening again. He hated the time difference. He wondered what he was going to do all day. It had to be something that would take his mind away from the Cominco email. He decided to go to the mall.

When he got to the mall, he moved aimlessly from one clothing store to another, taking his time. Before long, he got frustrated because he was seeing nice clothes that he could not afford. To make matters worse, he had no idea when he would be able to afford those clothes. Given his current situation he wondered if he would ever be able to afford those clothes. He gave up and went into a pub and started drinking. While drinking he got buried in thoughts, and before he realized it, it was time to go back home. He hoped Cominco would have replied his email by the time he got home.

Jill was already home from work.

"Hi, honey! How was your day?" he greeted his wife as he entered the kitchen.

"I am fine. How was your day? Did you get any reply from Cominco?"

"They hadn't replied when I checked in the morning. I am going to check now."

Zvina went upstairs to check his email. Yes, he had an email from Cominco's Human Resources Manager. He quickly opened it and started reading it. He was shaking as he read the email. Unfortunately, they had not changed their decision. They said they had filled the position already and did not have any suitable vacancies at this time. They encouraged him to apply in the future if suitable positions became available. This was a big blow to Zvina. He felt like a heavy cloud had landed on him and was engulfing him in hopelessness and misery.

"I knew it!" he shouted, banging the desk with a clenched fist.

"What is it?" asked Jill from downstairs. "What did they say?"

"They did not change their decision. They said the vacancy has been filled. I knew it! Since the whole thing started, something at the back of my mind kept telling me that it was not going to happen. Now here we are," said Zvina, getting up from the computer desk.

"Don't be pessimistic about life, honey! It was never meant to be your opportunity. Your opportunity will come."

"But Jill, look at this. It took over eight months to process a work permit. If one had to apply for a permit to go to heaven, I don't think it would take that long. There is something to this. I have bad luck. I shouldn't have told people that I got a job in Canada and I was applying for a work permit. Someone cast a spell of bad luck on me," said Zvina as he walked downstairs to the living room.

"No...no...no! Don't entertain such thoughts, honey. I told a lot of people about my work permit for the UK as well. Probably the same people that you told," Jill pointed out. She asked, "Why didn't they cast that spell on me?"

"You and I don't have the same totem. That person might not know how to appease your ancestors to get their juju to work on you."

"If you think like that, you will never get anywhere in life. That used to happen centuries ago, but not now. This opportunity was never meant for you. Forget it, and let's move on. Our permanent residency application for Canada is being processed. I am confident that we will not have any issues with that because we meet all of the requirements."

"You can be hopeful, but mind you, it's been over a year-and-a-half since we submitted our application. We haven't heard from them. Now I don't have faith in these things."

"You have to have faith. Anyway, if we don't get Canadian permanent residency, we will live here. There are lots of opportunities in the UK as well."

"Lots of opportunities? For you, not me. There is no mining industry here. There are no jobs for me," said Zvina in a tone of desperation.

"We can try Australia. It's a good country too. At that seminar we attended in Zimbabwe, they said that there is a big mining industry in Australia."

"I think we need to look into that as well. If we don't hear from the Canadians in the next six months, we should just apply for Australian residency. In the meantime, I must seriously look for something to do. I can't just sit here and rot."

Zvina decided to apply for any job. He just wanted to get out of the house.

Within a week, he got a job at a call centre selling insurance to senior citizens. Within the first hour on this job, he realized that this was not his kind of job. However, at this time he had no other options. He had to work there while he looked for another job. After two painful weeks of working at the call centre, he was relieved to get another job at a workshop where they repaired TV digital boxes. Although he preferred this job to the one at the call centre, this new job was more physically demanding. They worked standing all day, and he had to do some heavy lifting from time to time. This was not the type of work a person with an engineering degree would normally find themselves doing. At first Zvina resented this so badly that he kept to himself at work. He would only talk to his co-workers when it was absolutely necessary. Sometimes he would go back to his car during breaks and cry. With time, he came to terms with his situation and he opened up and started making friends at work. But he continued looking for a suitable job in his field.

Chapter Ten

The Interview that Never Happened

When Zvina returned home from work one Thursday, he picked up the mail from the mailbox. Then he went inside and sat down in the living room to read the mail. When he picked up the third letter, he was elated to find that it was from the Canadian Embassy in Buffalo, NY. After many months, they had finally sent him a letter. He could not wait to read what message the letter contained. All of a sudden, his joy turned into anxiety. As he held the letter, his hands started shaking. He was not ready to read the message yet. He put the letter back on the table, stood up, and started walking around the room. Looking up at the ceiling, he thought about all the possible messages that the letter might have and singled out what he thought would be the worst message for him. Obviously, the worst message would be, "Your application for permanent residency has been denied." He thought about his next steps if this was the message for him. That would mean he would stay in the UK and keep looking for a suitable job. Eventually, he would have to apply for permanent residency in Australia if he wanted to leave the UK. He thought for a while before sitting down. He picked up the letter and quickly opened it.

The message in the letter turned out to be one of the best things that had happened to Zvina since moving to the UK. The Canadian Embassy had scheduled an immigration interview for him and his wife in Buffalo in three months. That was very good news for Zvina. At least there was hope. He went to the kitchen and got a cold beer from the fridge.

"I should drink to this," he said to himself as he opened his bottle of beer. "After all these months? Oh my God. I didn't see this coming. Jesus is wonderful."

He could not wait to tell his wife. He called her at work, only to be reminded by the automated answering machine that the pharmacy had closed for the day. It was after six p.m. He put the phone down and went back to the kitchen to prepare dinner. Before doing anything in the kitchen, he changed his mind and decided that they would go to a restaurant instead. They had to celebrate the good news. He went back and sat down in the living room.

Before long, his wife was home.

"How was your day, honey?" he asked Jill as she closed the door behind her.

"My day was good. How was your day?"

"It was not one of the greatest days until I got home."

"Until you got home? What happened here? Or should I say what's happening here?" asked Jill anxiously.

"Well, we got a letter from the Canadian Embassy in Buffalo," replied Zvina.

"What did they say?" asked Jill.

"They want us to attend an interview in person in three months," said Zvina.

"Wow!! That's good news, indeed!" said Jill, kissing her husband before sitting down next to him. "I was beginning to lose hope. It's been over eighteen months since we submitted the application."

"Yes. I was beginning to lose hope too. For a few moments, I did not have the courage to open the letter. I was worried I would be disappointed," admitted Zvina.

"Well, we can still be optimistic," said Jill.

"There might be a bit of a hurdle, though," said Zvina, getting up to pour a glass of wine for his wife.

"What is it? There you go again with your pessimistic mind," admonished Jill.

"Here you are," Zvina handed his wife a glass of wine.

"What hurdle are you talking about?" Jill asked again.

"We will need to get visas to go to the U.S. It's not easy to get a U.S. visa."

"I know it's not easy, but with this letter as evidence that we have been invited by the Canadian Embassy, I don't think they will refuse us the visas. We live in the UK legally, and we are applying to live in Canada legally. Who would be stupid enough to live illegally in the US when they can live legally in Canada or the UK? To me that's a no-brainer. It's not like we are coming from a third world country."

"I hear you, but you never know with these people. Anyway, let's celebrate. I think we should treat ourselves to a good meal in a good restaurant tonight. What do you think?"

"It's Thursday, honey. We have to go to work in the morning. Why don't we do that tomorrow evening? That way we can have a few drinks too."

"But I haven't started making dinner yet."

"Ok. We can order pizza for delivery tonight. How is that?"

"Ok. You order the pizza then."

Jill ordered the pizza. While they were waiting for the pizza, they talked about a number of things including how they were missing their son. It was time to go to London and bring Fari home. They also talked about Jeni, who was still in detention. They would have to visit her if they decided to go and get Fari from London. Their challenge was the cost of daycare for Fari. They could not afford it. They decided to find out if it was possible for Jeni to come and stay with them while her asylum claim was being processed.

The next day Jill called the immigration detention centre to enquire about Jeni's situation. They told her that her asylum claim would take a long time to process. As a result, they had moved her from the detention centre to a private home in Sheffield. They gave her the address and the phone number. Jill was delighted to have this information. She immediately called the phone number and was even more delighted to speak with her sister. Apparently, she was staying less than twenty minutes away from where they lived. She told her that on the weekend they would come and visit her.

The following day, Zvina and Jill visited Jeni. When they got to the house, Jeni was there waiting for them. She screamed with joy upon seeing them. They greeted each other with long hugs before Jeni showed them into the house.

"Tell us," Jill began, "what's your story? What's going to happen to you? You did not tell me the full story when we spoke on the phone yesterday."

"It's a long story. I don't even know where to begin. Where is Fari?"

"Fari is in London with his grandmum," replied Zvina.

"I miss him. When are you going to bring him?"

"We are not sure yet. It's very expensive to have him in daycare here," said Jill. "We will talk about Fari later. First, I have been so worried about you. Tell us what's going on."

"Ok. I will tell you the whole story. I guess you are not in a hurry. Would you like something to eat or drink first?"

"We are ok, Jeni," said Zvina. "We had breakfast less than two hours ago."

"Ok. I will start from the time they took me to the detention centre just after you guys left."

Jeni narrated her ordeal to her two relatives. By all standards it was quite an ordeal, but she made it sound like fun and games. From time to time she would burst into laughter, to the amusement of Jill and Zvina who were touched by her story and felt sorry for her.

"After I got fed up with the treatment and thinking I was going to be deported even after what I had gone through, I just decided to claim political asylum. Another Zimbabwean lady I met at the detention centre had told me that she was going to claim political asylum. I got the idea from her. This lady told me that she would tell them that she was an MDC party supporter and that Zanu–PF supporters and government agents had threatened to kill her. So, I did the same. At that point, things took another turn, and here I find myself."

"So, what's going to happen to you?" asked Jill.

"I will stay here until my case goes to court. If my claim is successful, I will be granted refugee status. If it's not, then they will deport me."

"Do you know the court date?" asked Zvina.

"No. Some say it may take months, or even years," replied Jeni.

"What do you do in the meantime?" Zvina asked again.

"Nothing. They pay for my accommodation here and they give me a weekly living allowance."

"That would be a boring life," remarked Zvina.

"You can say that again, Zvina," said Jeni. "I am sick and tired of sitting around doing nothing already. Yet it's only been a few weeks since I moved here."

"They should give you some form of temporary visa so that you can find a job and work," said Jill. "Could you look for a job?"

"If they catch you, they will deny your claim and deport you."

After hearing Jeni's story, the three talked about many other topics ranging from life in Zimbabwe to the future. Zvina and Jill told Jeni about the recent development in their permanent residency application for Canada. They promised to help Jeni move to Canada if she was deported from the UK. They also talked about finding out if UK immigration would allow Jeni to move in with them while she was waiting for her case to go to court. If Jeni moved in with them, then they would bring Fari home since Jeni would be at home to babysit him. Jeni liked the idea and promised to find out if this could happen the following week.

"Ladies! We have been talking for more than two-and-a-half hours now. I am getting hungry," said Zvina, rubbing his tummy.

"I can make us lunch," offered Jeni, getting up.

"No thank you. Don't worry. Lunch is on me. I saw a restaurant down the road as we were coming here. I can't remember its name now."

"The Old Swan?" asked Jeni.

"Yes, that's it. Is it a good restaurant? We could go there for lunch."

"Asylum seekers don't have money to dine out," said Jeni, laughing. "I haven't been there yet."

"Ok. Let's try it," said Zvina, getting up.

"Do you stay by yourself here?" Jill asked Jeni.

"No. There are two other women. They went downtown."

The trio left the house and walked down the road to the Old Swan, an old style British neighbourhood restaurant. They liked it. Their menu offered meals for the not-so-hungry and the very hungry. The food was like home-cooked, of a very high standard, and reasonably priced. The ambience in the dining area was very inviting and the service was very good.

After their meal, on their way back to Jeni's place, a bus passed them. The bus was going to a local bus terminal, and so Zvina and Jill decided to catch the next bus to the bus terminal and transfer to their home bus route at the terminal. They waited for the bus at the next bus stop, which was close to Jeni's place. Before long, the bus arrived. Zvina and Jill bade Jeni farewell and hopped onto the bus.

When they got home, they called Zvina's mum and talked to her and Fari for some time. Fari did not want to get off the phone.

"Fari misses us. We have to go and get him soon," said Jill, after finally putting down the phone.

"You are right. I miss him too. Let's see what Jeni comes up with regarding moving in with us," replied Zvina.

"If they don't allow her to move in with us, I think we could ask her to come every weekday and spend the day here with Fari. She would not have a problem with that," Jill reasoned.

"For sure. Now we have to talk about applying for U.S. visas to attend the interview. The sooner we do it, the better," Zvina suggested.

"Yes, you are right. Do you know what we are supposed to do?" asked Jill.

"Yes. I found the information on their website. You have to get all the documents they need and then call them. They will give you a date when you have to bring your application along with the required documents," replied Zvina.

"What are the required documents?"

"Passports, obviously; proof of funds to support yourself while you are there; documents that support your reason for visiting; and airfare tickets."

"But how can you buy air tickets before you get the visas?" asked Jill, rather puzzled.

"Good question! It does not make sense. But I guess you can buy cancellation insurance in case they don't give you the visa," Zvina suggested.

"But still, the cancellation insurance is money you will lose for no good reason. They should just ask you to prove that you can afford the airfares," said Jill.

"Anyway, that's what their website says. I think I will ask them that question before I book the appointment," said Zvina.

"You should, because we don't want to end up losing money for nothing. Not that I am pessimistic, but just in case," said Jill.

"For sure. I think we have all the documents we need except the tickets. We have our passports with UK visas, we have bank statements to prove that we have money, and we have the letter from the Canadian Embassy. As a matter of fact, with this letter they should waive the need for some of these stupid documents," said Zvina.

A few days later, Jeni called Jill and told her that she would move in with them. Jill and Zvina were very pleased with this. That week Zvina took two days off and went to London to get Fari. When Zvina and Fari returned, Jeni had already moved in.

Shortly after dinner on the day they were supposed to travel to London to apply for the visas, Jill and Zvina went through their documents again (for the nth time) to confirm that they had all the documents that would be required at the U.S. Embassy for their visa application. Their appointment was at nine a.m. at the U.S. Embassy in London. Since Jill had only accrued one vacation day at work, she had to work on the day before their interview. They would have to travel to London overnight in order to get there in time for the interview.

"We are good, honey! We have everything we need," said Zvina to his wife before handing the documents back to her.

"Ok. What time should we call the cab?" asked Jill.

"I think we should call the cab one hour before bus departure. I know it only takes about twenty minutes to get to the bus terminal, but I am not taking any chances. I would rather wait at the bus terminal than miss the bus, because what if something happened on our way there and we got delayed?"

"I agree. Let's relax for now. I am very tired. It was very busy at work today. And I imagine I will not be having a proper sleep tonight."

Jill and Zvina joined Fari and Jeni who were watching TV in the living room.

"I think you should buy another TV," said Jeni, as Jill and Zvina sat down.

Zvina started laughing. "I think you are right. Only one person watches TV in this family. And unfortunately, we don't like his shows. Fari watches TV pretty much all day. He does not take a break from it."

Zvina crawled over and sat on the floor next to Fari, right in front of the TV.

"Fari, can we change the channel please? Give me the remote," said Zvina, trying to get the remote from Fari.

"No!" screamed Fari, clenching the remote tightly with both hands.

"I will take you to town for that ride if you give me the remote," Zvina said persuasively.

"No!" screamed Fari again.

"How about the computer? I can put on that show you like on the computer," said Zvina, standing up to go upstairs to the computer.

Fari threw the remote on the floor, grabbed his dad's hand, and started pulling him. "Let's go, Dad! Let's go! I like that show."

Zvina and Fari went upstairs. Jeni picked up the remote and changed the channel. Zvina and Fari watched cartoons on the Internet.

The Long Trip To Canada

After about an hour, it was time for Zvina and Jill to go. Jill called a taxi and Zvina put Fari to sleep. Within fifteen minutes, the cab arrived and Zvina and Jill left. They got to the terminal about thirty minutes before the departure time. They checked in and sat in the waiting area.

After what seemed like several hours of waiting, the bus finally arrived. The sleepy pair got on the bus and took their seats. They chatted a little, but by the time the bus departed, they had fallen asleep. It was a long and painful night. Along with the other passengers, they would fall asleep for about half an hour before waking up and spending the next half hour awake. The bus stopped at a couple of stations for fifteen minutes each time. By the time they arrived in Central London, traffic was starting to pick up. Zvina and Jill got off the bus and found a coffee shop so they could have breakfast while they waited for the American Embassy to open.

When they finished their breakfast, the American Embassy was still an hour and a half from opening. They wondered what they could do in the meantime. They could not just sit in the coffee shop doing nothing.

"Should we walk around and check out Central London? I am still not very familiar with it," asked Jill.

"Sounds like a good idea, but you know what? Let's just pass through the front of the Embassy and make sure we know our way back."

"Ok. Let's go."

They left the coffee shop and walked down the street to the American Embassy. When they got there, they were surprised to see a queue of people waiting at one of the entrances.

"Why are those people queuing there? That might be a queue of people wanting to apply for visas as well. Let's find out. We don't want to go away and come back to a longer queue. We might have to join the queue now," said Zvina, walking towards the queue.

"Good morning," Zvina greeted a lady that was in the queue. "What is this queue for?"

"It's for visa applications," replied the lady.

"Ok. Thank you very much," said Zvina. Turning to Jill, he said, "Honey, these people are waiting for visa applications. Let's join the queue."

After waiting for more than an hour, the embassy doors finally opened and the queuing people moved in. By that time there were over forty people in the queue and there were twelve people in front of Zvina and Jill. Although there were many people inside the Embassy hall where the queuing people were being served, it was very quiet. The only people that were talking were those being served. It was a very solemn environment.

"This is rather intimidating. No one looks happy in here. Everybody seems to be lost in deep thoughts about something. It almost feels as though one is not going to have a pleasant experience here," Zvina whispered to Jill.

"Shhhh," Jill shushed him down.

"Seriously! That is how I am beginning to feel now," Zvina whispered again.

"Be quiet. You don't want to be the only one talking."

From the time they entered the building, the queue moved pretty fast. Within forty-five minutes, it was Zvina and Jill's turn. They went to the available counter where they were greeted by a stern-looking male officer.

"Good morning. What brings you to the American Embassy? What can I do for you?"

"Good morning," replied Zvina, "We have an appointment to submit our application for visitors' visas to the USA."

"Ok. Do you have all the required documents and the fees?"

"Yes, we do."

"Ok. Can I have the documents first?"

Jill opened her handbag and pulled out the envelope containing the documents. She took the documents out and handed them to Zvina.

"Here you are, Sir," said Zvina, handing over the documents to the officer. "We are husband and wife so for some of the documents we just have one document for both of us."

"Ok. I will have a look at the documents," said the officer. He sat back down on the chair behind him.

The officer quickly perused through the documents before looking up to ask Zvina a question.

"Why are you in the UK? You are Zimbabwean."

"We work here. We have work visas," replied Zvina.

"How long have you lived in the UK?"

"About five months."

"Why do you want to go to the USA?"

"We applied for Canadian permanent residency thorough the Canadian Embassy in Buffalo, NY. They have asked us to come for an interview. That's where we want to go. The invitation letter is there among the documents I gave you."

"There is a Canadian Embassy here in London. Why did you choose the Canadian Embassy in Buffalo?"

"At the time we applied for permanent residency, I was looking for employment in Canada. If I had been successful in getting a job in Canada, that would have been one of the nearest Canadian embassies for me to attend an interview like this."

"Why then did you not apply through the immigration office in Canada?"

"You cannot apply through an office in Canada. You can only apply through an embassy outside of Canada," replied Zvina in a shaky voice. He was becoming irritated by the officer's questions.

"You have only lived in the UK for a short period of time. How do I know you will come back to the UK if I give you the visas?"

"We have applied for Canadian permanent residency. We wouldn't want to ruin our chances of getting it by breaking immigration laws," reasoned Zvina.

"Can you convince me that your intended final destination is Canada and not the USA?" asked the officer.

"We are both professionals. We know that if we live in a country illegally, we will not get jobs in our professions. We can find jobs in our professions here in the UK because we are living here legally. If we succeed in getting Canadian permanent residency, we will be able to find jobs in our professions in Canada. We do not have any intentions to live in the USA illegally. We do not want to do under the table mediocre jobs. It does not make sense."

"Is that right?" questioned the officer.

"Of course, Officer! Who would do that? The UK and Canada are first world countries, just like the USA. Why would we want to live in the U.S. illegally when we can live legally in the UK or Canada and have a good life?" retorted Zvina.

"Anyway, I get your point, but I will not let you enter the USA," stated the officer.

"Can you kindly explain to me why?" asked Zvina calmly.

"I am not convinced you will come back. You have not lived in the UK long enough. Go back to Zimbabwe and apply at the USA Embassy in Zimbabwe," said the officer.

"But Officer, I am living in the UK. Besides, it costs a lot to fly to Zimbabwe and back to the UK," pleaded Zvina.

"I am afraid that's what you are going to have to do," said the officer.

"Officer, I just don't understand this," said Zvina.

"I am done with you. Here are your documents," said the officer. He handed Zvina back his documents.

"Can I appeal this decision? Can I see your supervisor?" asked Zvina, now desperate.

"Sir, I have the authority to make this decision and no one can reverse it. Not even the Ambassador. Don't waste your time. Take your documents and go. I will not let you enter the USA." The officer was adamant.

Zvina picked up the documents and quietly walked away with his wife following behind. This was a big disappointment to them. As they walked out the door, Zvina felt like everyone in the building had seen what had just happened. He felt like everyone was looking at him and thinking what a loser he was. He felt his legs crumbling. He couldn't keep walking. He looked around for a place to sit, but before he could find a place to sit, the thought of people staring at him and calling him a loser consumed his mind. He had to leave the building as soon as possible. Within seconds they were out of the building.

"What do we do now?" asked Jill, when they got outside the building.

"I have never experienced anything like this. He would not even take the time to understand our situation," said Zvina.

"You know what? Just forget about that guy and let's move on. We need to think about our next move," concluded Jill.

"What time are we supposed to catch the bus back home?" asked Zvina.

"In three hours. We could find somewhere to sit and have coffee or we could do some window shopping. What would you prefer?" asked Jill.

"Whatever you prefer. I know you would prefer window shopping," said Zvina.

"Ok. Window shopping it is," said Jill, attempting to be cheerful.

After two hours of window shopping that turned into shopping, Jill ended up with a couple of shopping bags filled with new purchases.

"I am tired," said Zvina. "Let's find a fast food restaurant and have lunch. We have to be at the bus terminal fifteen minutes before departure."

After lunch, they went to the bus terminal and got on the bus going back to Sheffield.

When they got home, Jeni was watching TV while Fari lay on the floor playing with his little toys.

"How was your trip?" asked Jeni as Zvina and Jill entered.

"It was horrible," replied Jill. "How are you guys doing? Fari, can't you see that Mum and Dad are home?"

"Hi Mummy. Hi Daddy. Where have you been?"

"Did you get the visas?" asked Jeni.

"No. We didn't," replied Zvina. "The officer wouldn't even let us apply. The guy was very rude and wouldn't even allow me to explain why we need to visit the States."

"What are you going to do now?" asked Jeni.

"We will send a letter to the Canadian Embassy and explain why we can't attend the interview. We will request to have our file transferred to the Canadian Embassy in London," said Zvina.

"Won't that delay the process?" asked Jeni.

"Most definitely it will delay the process, but there is nothing else we can do," said Zvina.

First thing the next morning, Zvina sat down at his computer desk and typed a letter to the Canadian Embassy in Buffalo, New York:

Dear Sir / Madam,

My wife and I are scheduled to attend an interview on September 20, 2002. Unfortunately, I regret to inform you that we will not be able to attend the interview. We could not get visas to visit the USA. Based on the discussion that we had with an officer at the USA Embassy in London, it does not look like we will be able to get visitor visas to the USA in the near future. As a result, we would like to request that our application file be transferred to the Canadian Embassy in London. I hope this will be acceptable.

Regards,
Zvina Mawira

"Jill, please come and read this before I print it," Zvina asked Jill, who was getting ready to go to work.

"Ok. Let me just finish my makeup."

After finishing her makeup, Jill quickly read the letter and said she was ok with it. Zvina printed the letter and signed it. Then he took it to the post office where he mailed it by first class service.

Several weeks passed and they did not receive anything from the Canadian Embassy. During this period Zvina got a mineral processing engineering job in Castleford. The commute between Sheffield and Castleford was too much for Zvina, so they moved to Castleford. Since Lloyds Pharmacies chain had many pharmacies located all over the country, Jill got transferred to a pharmacy in a small village of Allerton Bywater just outside of Castleford. Jeni also moved with them.

Zvina and Jill sent the Canadian Embassy another letter to inform them of their change of address. They also set up mail redirection from their old address to their new address. They wanted to make sure that they would not lose any mail.

Two months after the interview date had passed, they received a letter from the Canadian Embassy. To their disappointment, the Canadian Embassy had not transferred their file to their London office. Instead, they had rescheduled the interview to February 20, 2003.

"This is ridiculous," said Zvina after reading the letter. "I thought it was very clear in our letter that we were requesting to have our file transferred. Why would they reschedule the interview in the U.S. when we told them we cannot get U.S. visas?"

"I wonder if we can request to have the interview done in London but not necessarily move the file," said Jill.

"I don't know. I will have to write to them and ask," said Zvina, wearily.

"Maybe that's what we will have to do," offered Jill.

"I will waste no time. Let me draft the letter now and post it tomorrow. The interview date is just over two months away," said Zvina. He went upstairs and wrote another letter.

Dear Sir / Madam,

We received a letter that states that our interview has been rescheduled to February 20, 2003. However, in our letter dated June 23, 2002 we had informed you that we cannot get visas to travel to the USA. As a result, we were requesting to have our application file transferred to the Canadian Embassy in London. If the file cannot be transferred, is it possible to attend the interview at the Canadian Embassy in London? We would really appreciate your help and guidance on this important matter, because it is impossible for us to get visas to visit the USA.

Regards,

Zvina Mawira

Once again Zvina printed, signed, and posted the letter by first class mail service.

Several months passed and Zvina and his family did not hear anything from the Canadian Embassy. One day when Zvina got back from his business trip in Africa, Jill picked him up from Leeds Airport. Zvina had been gone for two weeks, and he wondered if Jill had received any news from the Canadian Embassy while he was gone.

"Any letter from the Canadian Embassy?" he asked as Jill merged onto the highway.

"No. We did not receive anything from them," Jill answered.

"I think they transferred our file to London. We are supposed to be hearing from the London office," said Zvina.

"But don't you think they are supposed to notify us that the file has been transferred and we will be dealing with the London office going forward?" asked Jill.

"I think they should, but it might be something they just do without notifying us. The office where the file has been transferred will contact the applicant once they have received and reviewed the file. I think that's what's happening here," reasoned Zvina.

"Well, you know how in the past I have been more optimistic about this application than you? Now I think it's the opposite. Every day that passes by without us receiving a letter from the Canadians makes me lose hope," admitted Jill.

"Me too, but I have realized that this is a very slow process. I think that when we send them correspondence, they do not review it and take action right away. I think they just put it in our file and leave it in the queue until its scheduled review date," said Zvina.

"I hear what you are saying, but I think it's time we start living our lives and forget this thing. Our lives are on hold now because of this. We are not settled here in the UK. We are not doing things we should be doing because we keep saying we are moving to Canada. It's been over a year and a half since we moved to the UK. Now Fari is four. We do not have a second child, because we wanted to wait until we go to Canada. Now there will be a big age difference between our kids because we have had to wait so long hoping to go to Canada. I am getting sick and tired of this. Let's carry on with our lives, and whatever happens to the application for permanent residency in Canada, we will not regret wasting valuable time in our lives," said Jill passionately.

The Long Trip To Canada

"It's just that we need to have permanent residency status and eventually citizenship in the country we live in. We do not have permanent residency status or citizenship in the UK. If you cannot renew your work permit when it expires, we will have to leave. I don't want to have to go back to Zimbabwe if that was to happen. But I agree with you. We should move on. We should plan to have our second child by summer next year. Then there will only be a five-year age difference between our kids. I don't want it to be more than that. I think they should grow up together and enjoy childhood together," said Zvina.

"We've even held off from purchasing household furniture. I want quality furniture, but we keep saying we can't buy quality furniture because we will have to sell it cheap and lose money when we move to Canada. We should just get settled here and enjoy our lives," Jill emphasized again, as she exited highway M1 onto highway M62 towards Castleford. "Let's discuss this before we go to bed tonight."

When they got home Fari was fast asleep in the back seat. Zvina picked him up and took him inside while Jill carried Zvina's luggage. Jeni was in the kitchen preparing dinner. Zvina took a quick shower and then joined Jill and Jeni for dinner.

Later that night when Jill and Zvina were getting ready to go to bed, they resumed their conversation.

"Like we discussed this afternoon, we have to carry on with our lives whether we end up moving to Canada or not," Jill began.

"I totally agree," said Zvina, nodding.

"Let's plan on having our second child next summer. Do you agree?" asked Jill.

"Yes, I do. Remember, before we had Fari our family plan was to have two kids that were two years apart. Fari is four now, so we did not achieve our plan, but we still need two kids. We should not wait any longer," said Zvina.

"Ok. I will stop using birth control immediately. You never know; it might take a couple of months or so for me to conceive," said Jill with a tremble in her voice.

Zvina stared at Jill for a moment. He smiled and kissed Jill and said, "Sure. Stop birth control immediately."

"How about things I want for the house like furniture, kitchen utensils, and other little things to make this house comfortable?" asked Jill.

"You can start buying the things you want. However, I think we should not buy anything on credit. We can use money from our savings. If it's not enough, we can use some of the money we saved as settling funds in Canada," suggested Zvina.

"Ok. I want to start enjoying life here. Just wait and see. I will furnish this house with quality furniture. I know you don't like shopping, but I think for big things like bedroom and living room furniture we have to go shopping together. I want you to help me decide. For the dining room and kitchen stuff, Jeni can help me out," said Jill.

"Sure," said Zvina.

"When we start furnishing our house, people will ask if we have given up on moving to Canada. What will we tell them?" asked Jill as she joined Zvina in bed.

"I will just tell them the truth. The application has taken too long, and so we have decided to move on and enjoy our lives here. If we end up getting Canadian residency later in the coming months or years, then we will make a decision to either move or stay in the UK at that time. Right now, we have chosen to live a normal life and get settled in the UK. We both have good jobs now. We can live comfortably here for the next few years," said Zvina, comfortingly.

"You are right. The only difference is that in Canada we would have permanent residency, while here in the UK, I have to renew my work permit every three years. As long as I can renew my work permit, we can have a good life in the UK. Hey!! You are falling asleep!" said Jill, nudging Zvina's shoulder.

"Yes, honey. I am tired. You know it's a long flight from Johannesburg to Amsterdam and then connecting from Amsterdam to Leeds," said Zvina.

"I know. Sometimes I feel sorry for you. You travel too much. Anyway, good night," said Jill, kissing Zvina.

"Good night."

Within a few minutes Zvina was fast asleep and snoring. Jill pushed and turned him over into a position where he would not snore. Jill did not fall asleep right away. She pondered over what they had discussed on their way home from the airport and just minutes ago. She thought about what having a second child involved. A new baby would mean that she would have to take maternity leave for at least six months. That would mean a reduction in their income for that duration, as she would not be entitled to full pay. She thought they were not ready to take a cut in their income at that time, especially given that she would be using most of their savings to buy furniture for the house. She decided that they could delay having the second child by six months.

Once Zvina woke up the next morning, Jill was ready to tell him what she had decided overnight.

"Honey, I did some thinking after our discussion last night. I think we should hold off on having a second child for the next six months."

"Why?" asked Zvina, lifting his head up off the pillow.

"We agreed that we have to buy good furniture for our house; that means we will be using a lot of money from our savings. When I go on maternity leave, I am not entitled to full pay, so then we will have less income during that time. I wouldn't want us to have a second child at a time when we don't have much in our savings. I suggest that we furnish the house now and save for the next ten to fifteen months before I go on maternity leave. By that time, we should have a good amount in our savings to prepare for the arrival of the new child in a comfortable home. What do you think?"

"Actually, that's a good idea. We will need money to buy stuff for the new kid and for any emergencies that might arise during that time. I agree with you."

"So, I will stay on birth control for the next six months, and then after I get pregnant I will have another seven or eight months to work. By then, we should have some good savings. Deal?" asked Jill, shaking Zvina's hand.

"Deal," replied Zvina. "You are a smart woman. That's why I love you."

"Good morning, Dad. Good morning, Mum. Good morning, me," said Fari, jumping onto his parents' bed.

"Good morning, Fari," Jill and Zvina said at the same time.

"Ok, people. Let's get up and go and make breakfast," said Jill, jumping out of bed.

Chapter Eleven

Canada! Here We come!

In the days following Jill and Zvina's decision to move on and enjoy life in the UK, their lifestyle took a significant turn. Jill went on a shopping spree and furnished the house. They sold their old car and bought a newer one. They made more friends and hosted barbeques for their new friends and relatives regularly. They went out on weekends more often. This was the kind of lifestyle they had been used to back in Zimbabwe. There were many Zimbabweans that lived in the nearby city of Leeds and Zvina and Jill had made friends with some of them. They had also known some of them before they moved to the UK. At that time Zvina and Jill felt they had finally settled in the UK, and they were happy about it. They rarely talked or even thought about their application for permanent residency in Canada. They had given up.

One evening when Zvina got back home from work, he picked up mail from the mailbox as usual. He went into the living room and placed the mail on the coffee table and started going through it. To his surprise, there was a letter from the Canadian Embassy in Buffalo, NY. He quickly opened the envelope and read the letter. He could not believe what he was reading. He thought he must be dreaming. He put the letter on the coffee table and rushed into the bathroom to splash cold water on his face. He went back into the living room, picked up the letter, and read it again. After rereading the letter, he threw the letter back on the coffee table, sighed, and threw himself onto the sofa. He jumped up, picked up the letter again, and called Jeni.

"Jeni! Jeni!" he yelled. "Come here. Come and read this."

"What is it?" asked Jeni, as she entered the living room.

"Read this. It's from the Canadian Embassy," said Zvina, handing the letter to Jeni.

Zvina then ran across the room and picked up Fari, who was lying on the floor watching TV. He came back and stood right in front of Jeni, watching her reading the letter.

"What?" yelled Jeni. "They have waived your interview? This is unbelievable. God is great."

"I can't believe this. I am in shock right now," said Zvina, snatching the letter from Jeni.

"It's hard to believe that they would waive the interview just like that after all this time," said Jeni.

"When I read this for the first time I thought I was dreaming. Honestly, I had to go to the bathroom to wash my face. I could not believe this. I can't wait to tell Jill. What time is it? She must be on her way home."

"She is going to jump through the roof once she hears this. Somebody better hold her down when you tell her," said Jeni.

Before long, Jill came home. As she entered the living room, Zvina threw the letter at her.

"What is it?" said Jill, as she picked up the letter.

"It's for you. Read it," said Zvina.

Jill calmly walked over to the sofa where Zvina was sitting and sat down next him. She opened the letter and started reading it.

"What? Please stop kidding me," said Jill. She stood up and looked up at the ceiling.

"No one is kidding you," said Jeni, laughing.

"After all this? After all this time? Somebody has got to be kidding."

Zvina stood up as well and hugged Jill.

"It's real, Jill. Canada, here we come," said Zvina.

"I can't believe this. This is just unbelievable. I never thought they would do something like that. I did not know they could waive immigration interviews. I thought they were mandatory," said Jill.

"Me neither," said Zvina. "I thought if an applicant failed to attend the interview for whatever reason, it was an automatic rejection."

"God is wonderful. I had given up on this. Let's all kneel and pray. We must thank God for this. It's a miracle. Come on, Fari," said Jill. She walked up to Fari, who was obviously oblivious to what was happening. He was busy playing with his little toy cars.

They all knelt and Jill prayed.

"Lord Almighty, thank you for the wonderful things you do in our lives. With you, dear Lord, all things are possible. We never thought this day would come upon us. We had given up on getting Canadian permanent residency. We thought the devil had won this battle. We were wrong, because your time had not come. Now, your time has come. Your will has been done. We thank you for fighting the battle for us behind

the scenes. As we celebrate today, let us not forget these good things you always do in our lives. Thank you, Lord. In the name of Jesus. Amen!"

"Thanks for the prayer, Jill," said Zvina. "We are immensely grateful."

"The next step is to go for medical examinations. We have to book our medicals ASAP. No time to waste," said Jill.

"Yes. I will call the doctor tomorrow and book appointments for the three of us."

"This calls for celebration. Jeni, don't make dinner. We will go out for dinner today," said Jill.

She picked up her handbag and went into the bedroom.

This latest development meant that Zvina and Jill had to revise their plans. Later that evening before they went to sleep, Zvina started the conversation.

"Jill, this new development means we have to revise our plans and change them as required."

"You are right. I think we should stop acquiring more stuff for the house," Jill suggested.

"What are you going to do with the expensive furniture that we have already? We cannot take it to Canada," asked Zvina.

"We can sell it. It shouldn't be hard to sell. The only thing is that we will sell them at a loss," said Jill.

"Would you rather ship our new furniture to Canada?" asked Zvina.

"I wouldn't ship furniture. I think we can sell it. It won't be a very big loss," said Jill confidently.

"Ok. How about having a baby? You are supposed to stop birth control at the end of this month. If we have a baby before we move to Canada, we will have to apply for a visa for the baby to enter Canada with us. That might be another lengthy process," perceived Zvina.

"I think it will be. Let's hold off until we move to Canada then," said Jill.

"Yes. Let's do that," agreed Zvina.

"But we don't have to wait until we get to Canada for me to stop using birth control. I can stop birth control when they ask us to send our passports to them for the visas. That way I might be pregnant by the time we move to Canada and our kid will be born soon after our arrival in Canada," offered Jill.

"Sounds like a plan," Zvina agreed.

In the days that followed, Zvina and his family booked appointments for the medical examinations and had the medicals done. After that it was just a waiting game.

Since Zvina and his family had not gone back to Zimbabwe since they had first left two years prior, they were homesick. They wanted to go back for Christmas this year. One evening, while they were watching TV after dinner, Jill started the discussion about going back to Zimbabwe for Christmas.

"Honey! It's been two years since we left Zimbabwe. I think we should go back for Christmas this year," Jill stated.

"I agree with you. I am very homesick too. I miss everyone there," replied Zvina.

"So, should we start booking our tickets now? It's three months away. But the sooner we buy the tickets, the better, because as we get closer to Christmas, they get more expensive," Jill noted.

"Sure. Let's search around and buy the tickets this month," suggested Zvina.

"How long do you think we should stay? I can take a full month off," said Jill.

"I only have three weeks of vacation remaining. We can stay for three weeks there," said Zvina.

"Ok. Which dates?" asked Jill, eager to set their plans in motion.

"I have to be back to work on January second. We will have to be back in the UK before January first, so that I can have a day to rest before going back to work," said Zvina.

"Ok. Three weeks in Zimbabwe, and then we will fly back on December thirtieth so you can have two days to rest. How is that?" asked Jill.

"I am ok with that," said Zvina.

Later that week Jill booked their flights to Zimbabwe and paid for the tickets. They would fly to Zimbabwe at the end of the first week of December, and then fly back to the UK on December thirtieth. Jill and Zvina were very excited. They started buying gifts for people back in Zimbabwe. They bought all sorts of gifts ranging from clothes to cellphones. In Zimbabwe, when you come back home from overseas, it is customary to bring gifts to your close relatives. Because Jill and Zvina had two extended families to bring gifts for, they ended up with so much luggage that they had to ship some of it by cargo.

One week before their scheduled flight to Zimbabwe, they received a letter from the Canadian Embassy. They had been granted permanent residency in Canada. The next step was for them to send their passports to the Embassy, so they could have visas issued.

The Long Trip To Canada

"Wow! Finally, we reach the end of the road. I don't know what to say. GOD IS WONDERFUL," said Zvina, as he handed the letter to Jill.

Jill received the letter and read it quietly.

"You are shaking!" exclaimed Zvina.

Jill's hands were visibly shaking. She did not reply, but soon after she finished reading the letter, she turned around and hugged her husband. She started crying.

"Why are you crying?" asked Zvina, trying to free himself from Jill's hug.

Jill did not answer. She placed her head against Zvina's chest and cried even louder. Zvina started patting her on the back and tried to calm her down.

Fari, who had not been paying attention to his parents, heard his mum crying. He stopped playing with his little cars, looked up, and watched them for a moment. When his mum continued crying, he stood up and went to join them in the hug. Realizing that Fari had joined them in the hug, Jill stopped crying.

"What is it, Mum?" asked Fari, looking up at his mum's face.

"Nothing, Fari. You won't understand," replied Jill.

"Mum is crying because she is very happy. You cry when you are sad, right?" said Zvina.

"Yes," said Fari, nodding.

"That's right. Kids cry when they are sad, but adults cry when they are happy. Mum is happy because we just learned that we will be going to live in Canada. She is happy we are moving to Canada. That's why she is crying."

"Ok, Daddy."

"You may go play with your toys."

Fari went back to play with his toys while Jill and Zvina sat on the couch next to each other.

"It's good that we have finally come to the end of this with a positive outcome," said Zvina. "Pass me the letter again. Does it say when we have to send our passports to the Embassy?"

Jill opened the letter again and scanned through it.

"It just says we have to send our passports to their offices immediately," said Jill.

"Then once again, we have a bit of a problem," said Zvina.

"What problem?" asked Jill.

"We are supposed to go to Zimbabwe in just over a week from now. We need our passports to travel outside of the UK. If we go to Zimbabwe, we cannot send our passports to the Canadian Embassy until we come back. That's a month away, and by then I think it will be too late for us to send our passports," said Zvina carefully.

"You know what? I was not even thinking about that. What do we do? I want to go to Zimbabwe this Christmas," said Jill.

"I want to send the passports right away. I don't want to lose this opportunity. It's been a long and painful journey to get where we are now. Did you buy cancellation insurance for the tickets? We can cancel our trip to Zimbabwe. We can always go after we get our passports back. It won't be Christmas time, but at least we will be one hundred percent sure that we have Canadian residency and we will have no need to worry about it anymore," said Zvina, taking the letter from Jill.

"No. I didn't buy cancellation insurance. We never discussed it and we had made up our minds that we were definitely going. Cancellation was not an option," Jill informed Zvina.

"Could we negotiate with the airline, and change our travelling dates?" asked Zvina.

"I am not sure if they would do that for us. I can find out," offered Jill.

"Ahhh! I know what we can do. We can use emergency travel documents. We will go to the Zimbabwean Embassy and explain exactly what happened and why we do not have our passports. I think they will give us emergency travel documents," suggested Zvina.

"Do you think so?" asked Jill, hesitantly.

"Yes. We will bring all of our correspondence with the Canadian Embassy as well as the tickets for the flights to Zimbabwe. If we show them all that, I think they will give us emergency travel documents."

"Ok. That's what we will do. You post the passports tomorrow, on Saturday. On Monday or Tuesday, we will go to London to get the emergency travel documents," confirmed Jill.

Three months later, Zvina and his family finally left the UK for Canada. They decided to land in Vancouver because Muko had already settled in Vancouver in British Columbia. He had extended an offer to Zvina and his family to stay with him while Zvina looked for a job and their own place. Zvina had accepted the offer.

When the plane landed in Vancouver, Zvina's mind raced. His past two experiences entering Canada had not been good at all. He wondered what would happen this time around. They had permanent residency visas stamped in their passports, and they had all the other necessary documents. But

Zvina still felt apprehensive about the impending encounter with immigration officials. He thought about the various possibilities. As they stepped out of the plane, Jill noticed that Zvina seemed anxious and rather nervous.

"What is it? You look nervous," Jill asked Zvina.

"I just don't trust the immigration officers. I hope they will not give us a hard time," replied Zvina.

"Why would they give us a hard time? We have the visas and everything else that is required," reasoned Jill.

"I know, but it's just a feeling I have. We will see," said Zvina, rather pessimistically.

When they arrived at the immigration desk, they handed over their passports to the officer. After checking the passports for a few minutes, the officer looked up and smiled at them.

"Congratulations, and welcome to Canada!" said the officer. He stood up and offered his handshake to the Mawiras.

"Thank you," replied Zvina.

"Follow me," the officer said, leading the Mawiras away. "We have to complete some paperwork before we let you go and celebrate your arrival in Canada. Do you have relatives or friends in Vancouver already?"

"Yes, we have a friend," replied Zvina.

"That's awesome! Is your friend at the airport waiting for you?" asked the officer.

"Yes," replied Jill.

The officer took the Mawiras to an office where they were asked to complete and sign a few forms. The officers were very friendly and made the whole process simple.

Zvina looked at his little family, and then closed his eyes for a moment in gratitude. This was a memorable occasion for the Mawiras. After almost four years, they had finally reached the end of their long trip to Canada.

Acknowledgements

I would like to thank my wife Josephine and my kids Tadiwanashe and Tamudasihe, for without their encouragement, this book would not have been written. I thank them for allowing me to spend many hours working on this book when I could have otherwise spent quality time with them. I cannot thank my wife enough for the amount of time she spent editing this book. Her suggestions have made this book what it is. I also thank her for travelling on this road with me. Without her, this long trip to Canada would not have been possible, and we would not have this story to tell. My friends Ridge Nyashanu, Michael Kuwani, and the late Tendai Mapaso deserve a million thanks for cheering me on. Last but not least, special mention goes to my uncle Billiard Kadungure for his encouragement. This was truly a worthwhile trip!

About the Author

Everest Siwira was born in Bulawayo, Zimbabwe. He holds a BSc (Hons) Metallurgical Engineering degree from the University of Zimbabwe. He also has an MBA from the Athabasca University, Alberta, Canada. He is a member of the Professional Engineers Association of Alberta and a licensed Financial Advisor with Alberta Insurance Council. He is married to Josephine and they have two sons, Tadiwanashe and Tamudaishe. They live in Alberta where Everest currently works in the Oil and Gas industry.